Biscuits and Gravy Cookbook
Irresistible Biscuit and Gravy Recipes for Every Occasion

BISCUITS AND GRAVY COOKBOOK

First edition. October 27, 2023.

Copyright © 2023 john ahmad.

ISBN: 979-8223491866

Written by john ahmad.

John Ahmad

Outline:

Introduction to Biscuits and Gravy

- History and origins
- Tips for making perfect biscuits and gravy

Biscuit Basics

- Classic buttermilk biscuits
- Flavored variations (cheddar, herbs, etc.)
- Gluten-free and vegan options

Gravy Galore

- Traditional sausage gravy
- Vegetarian and vegan gravy alternatives
- Flavorful regional variations

Biscuit Sandwiches

- Classic sausage and egg biscuit
- Southern fried chicken biscuit
- Veggie and cheese biscuit sliders

Biscuits with a Twist

- Biscuit breakfast casserole
- Biscuit waffles and pancakes
- Biscuit and gravy pot pie

International Biscuit Delights

- British scones with clotted cream
- Indian biscuits with spiced gravy

- Australian "damper" bread with bush gravy

Sweet Biscuit Treats

- Honey butter biscuits
- Berry-filled biscuits with glaze
- Cinnamon sugar biscuit bites

Savory Gravy Creations

- Mushroom and onion gravy
- Bacon and shallot gravy
- Roasted red pepper gravy

Biscuit Breakfast Bowls

- Biscuits and sausage gravy bowl
- Biscuit Benedict with poached eggs
- Veggie-loaded biscuit bowl

Gourmet Biscuit Meals

- Lobster bisque over biscuits
- Filet mignon and red wine gravy
- Spinach and artichoke biscuits

Biscuit Desserts

- Peach cobbler with biscuit topping
- Chocolate-stuffed biscuits
- Berry shortcakes

Hearty Gravy Combos

- Country fried steak with creamy gravy
- Biscuit shepherd's pie
- Turkey and stuffing biscuits

Quick and Easy Biscuits

- Biscuit in a mug (microwave recipe)
- Biscuit flatbreads
- Biscuit dumplings for stews

Sausage Variations

- Spicy chorizo gravy
- Maple breakfast sausage biscuits
- Italian sausage and peppers gravy

Biscuits for Special Diets

- Keto-friendly almond flour biscuits
- Paleo sweet potato biscuits
- Gluten-free biscuits and mushroom gravy

Gravy for Every Occasion

- Holiday turkey gravy
- Game day chili gravy
- Elegant wine and shallot gravy

Biscuit Brunch Ideas

- Biscuit and gravy bar
- Biscuit French toast

- Biscuit breakfast tacos

Vegetarian and Vegan Biscuit Feasts

- Vegan sausage and mushroom gravy
- Spinach and feta stuffed biscuits
- Lentil and vegetable biscuits

Biscuit Baking Troubleshooting

- Common biscuit mistakes and fixes
- Perfecting your gravy consistency

Biscuits and Gravy Beyond Breakfast

- Creative lunch and dinner ideas
- Leftover makeovers
- Freezing and reheating tips

Chapter 1: Introduction to Biscuits and Gravy

1.1 The Heritage of Biscuits and Gravy

Tracing the origins of biscuits: A global perspective

Biscuits, in their various forms, have a long and storied history that dates back centuries. The word "biscuit" itself has its origins in Latin, derived from the words "bis" (twice) and "coctus" (cooked). Early biscuits were not the flaky, buttery treats we know today but were hard, unleavened bread-like cakes that were baked twice to ensure their longevity.

As trade routes expanded, the concept of biscuits spread across continents, with various cultures adopting and adapting the simple yet versatile baked goods to their tastes and preferences. The Egyptians enjoyed hardtack biscuits made from barley and emmer wheat, while the ancient Greeks and Romans relished their version of savory biscuits flavored with spices and cheese.

The evolution of gravy: From medieval to modern

Gravy, on the other hand, has its roots in medieval Europe. The term "gravy" is believed to come from the Old French word "gravé," meaning "thickened." In medieval cooking, gravies were initially used to moisten and flavor dishes, but over time, they developed into rich, flavorful sauces, often made from the drippings of roasted meats.

As the art of sauce-making progressed, gravies became a central element of culinary traditions worldwide, incorporating various ingredients like herbs, spices, and liquids to create a wide range of flavors and textures.

1.2 Biscuits and Gravy in America

Southern influences on the biscuit tradition

When European settlers arrived in the New World, they brought their biscuit-making techniques with them. The southern United States, with its favorable climate for wheat cultivation and abundant dairy resources, became a hotbed for biscuit-making. Southern biscuits evolved to include leavening agents such as baking soda and baking powder, giving rise to the light, fluffy biscuits we know today.

The rise of sausage gravy as a popular pairing

Sausage gravy, a quintessential companion to biscuits in the South, has its own unique story. As the region was known for its pork production, sausage quickly became a common breakfast staple. Combining the savory goodness of sausage with a creamy, peppery gravy proved to be an irresistible match for tender, buttery biscuits. This hearty and satisfying breakfast dish gained popularity not only in the South but across the entire nation.

1.3 Iconic Regional Variations

Biscuits and red-eye gravy in the Appalachian region

In the Appalachian region of the United States, a distinct version of biscuits and gravy emerged, known as "red-eye gravy." This simple yet flavorful gravy is made by deglazing a pan used to cook country ham with black coffee. The result is a unique, tangy, and smoky sauce that pairs wonderfully with homemade biscuits, providing a delightful twist on the classic combination.

Biscuits and chocolate gravy in the Ozarks

Venturing to the Ozark region, we discover another fascinating variation of biscuits and gravy that takes a sweet turn. Here, biscuits are served with a delectable chocolate gravy made from cocoa powder, sugar, milk, and a touch of butter. This delightful treat is a testament to the versatility of biscuits and gravy, showing that they can be equally delightful as a sweet, dessert-like dish.

1.4 Biscuits and Gravy Across Cultures

The British biscuit and its journey to the United States

The British version of biscuits is more akin to what Americans know as cookies—crisp, sweet treats that are often enjoyed with a cup of tea. These biscuits made their way to the United States through early European settlers, but their transformation into flaky, tender biscuits is a distinctively American adaptation. Despite their differences, both British biscuits and American biscuits share a heritage that spans the Atlantic.

Gravy's diverse interpretations around the world

As biscuits traveled across borders, they encountered an array of gravies, each tailored to the unique tastes of different cultures. From rich, meaty gravies in Europe to spicy, aromatic gravies in Asia, the art of sauce-making became a reflection of the world's diverse culinary traditions. Biscuits and gravy, in their myriad forms, have become a testament to the universal love for comfort foods that bring warmth and satisfaction to the table.

With our historical exploration complete, we can now turn our attention to the heart of this cookbook—unleashing the delicious possibilities of biscuits and gravy in all their glory. Get ready to embark on a gastronomic adventure that celebrates the comforting and delightful world of Biscuits and Gravy!

Chapter 2: Biscuit Basics

Biscuits are the foundation of every great biscuits and gravy dish. In this chapter, we'll dive into the art of creating perfect biscuits—light, flaky, and buttery—every time. From classic buttermilk biscuits to exciting flavored variations and accommodating dietary preferences with gluten-free and vegan options, we've got you covered!

2.1 Classic Buttermilk Biscuits

There's something timeless and comforting about classic buttermilk biscuits. These golden delights are a blank canvas for a variety of toppings and gravies, making them a versatile staple in any kitchen. To create the ultimate classic buttermilk biscuit, follow these simple steps:

Ingredients:

- 2 cups all-purpose flour
- 1 tablespoon baking powder
- 1/2 teaspoon baking soda
- 1 teaspoon salt
- 6 tablespoons cold unsalted butter, cut into small cubes
- 1 cup buttermilk

Instructions:

1. Preheat your oven to 450°F (230°C) and line a baking sheet with parchment paper.
2. In a large mixing bowl, whisk together the flour, baking powder, baking soda, and salt.
3. Add the cold butter cubes to the dry ingredients and use a

pastry cutter or your fingertips to work the butter into the flour until the mixture resembles coarse crumbs.

4. Gradually pour in the buttermilk, stirring with a fork until the dough just comes together.
5. Turn the dough out onto a lightly floured surface and gently knead it a few times until it forms a cohesive ball.
6. Pat the dough into a circle about 3/4-inch thick. Use a biscuit cutter or a glass to cut out biscuits, and place them on the prepared baking sheet.
7. Bake the biscuits for 12 to 15 minutes or until they are golden brown on top.
8. Serve these classic buttermilk biscuits warm, slathered with butter and your favorite jam, or use them as the base for delicious biscuits and gravy combinations.

2.2 Flavored Variations

While classic buttermilk biscuits are wonderful on their own, experimenting with flavored variations can take your biscuit game to a whole new level. Here are some mouthwatering options to try:

a. Cheddar and Chive Biscuits:

Add 1 cup of shredded cheddar cheese and 2 tablespoons of chopped fresh chives to the dry ingredients before incorporating the butter and buttermilk. Proceed with the rest of the recipe as usual.

b. Rosemary and Garlic Biscuits:

Mix 1 tablespoon of finely chopped fresh rosemary and 1 teaspoon of garlic powder into the dry ingredients before adding the butter and buttermilk.

c. Sweet Honey Biscuits:

For a delightful sweet treat, replace 2 tablespoons of granulated sugar for a slightly sweeter biscuit. Drizzle honey over the biscuits before serving.

Experiment with different flavor combinations to find your favorite, and don't be afraid to get creative!

2.3 Gluten-Free and Vegan Options

Dietary restrictions should never stand in the way of enjoying delicious biscuits. Here are recipes for gluten-free and vegan biscuits that retain the delectable taste and texture of traditional biscuits:

Gluten-Free Biscuits:

Ingredients:

- 2 cups gluten-free all-purpose flour blend
- 1 tablespoon baking powder
- 1/2 teaspoon baking soda
- 1 teaspoon salt
- 6 tablespoons cold vegan butter or coconut oil (for dairy-free

option)

- 1 cup dairy-free buttermilk (made with almond milk and 1 tablespoon of lemon juice)

Instructions:

1. Follow the same instructions as the classic buttermilk biscuits, using gluten-free all-purpose flour and dairy-free buttermilk.

Vegan Biscuits:
Ingredients:

- 2 cups all-purpose flour
- 1 tablespoon baking powder
- 1/2 teaspoon baking soda
- 1 teaspoon salt
- 6 tablespoons cold vegan butter or coconut oil
- 1 cup almond milk (or any other plant-based milk) + 1 tablespoon of lemon juice

Instructions:

1. Follow the same instructions as the classic buttermilk biscuits, using vegan butter and almond milk with lemon juice to create the dairy-free buttermilk substitute.

2.4 Tips and Troubleshooting

To ensure your biscuits always turn out perfectly, follow these tips:

Use cold butter and buttermilk: Keeping the butter and buttermilk cold ensures flaky biscuits.

Handle the dough gently: Overworking the dough can make the biscuits tough. Knead it just enough to bring it together.

Don't twist the cutter: When cutting out the biscuits, press the cutter straight down without twisting to help them rise evenly.

Space biscuits properly: Leave a little space between the biscuits on the baking sheet to allow for even baking.

Adjust oven temperature and time: If your biscuits are browning too quickly, reduce the oven temperature slightly or cover them with foil.

Troubleshooting:

Flat biscuits: Overly soft dough or not enough leavening agents can cause biscuits to spread. Make sure your dough has the right consistency and that you've used enough baking powder and baking soda.

Tough biscuits: Overworking the dough or using too much flour can lead to tough biscuits. Handle the dough gently and measure the flour accurately.

Dry biscuits: Biscuits can become dry if they're overbaked or if there's too little fat. Keep an eye on them in the oven, and make sure you're using enough butter or vegan fat.

With these tips and tricks, you're ready to create delicious classic buttermilk biscuits and explore exciting flavored variations, all while accommodating gluten-free and vegan dietary needs. The biscuit possibilities are endless, and they'll serve as the perfect base for the hearty gravies we'll explore in the upcoming chapters. So, let's roll up our sleeves and continue our culinary journey through the world of Biscuits and Gravy!

Chapter 3: Gravy Galore

In this chapter, we'll dive into the wonderful world of gravies that pair so beautifully with biscuits. From the classic and hearty sausage gravy to delectable vegetarian and vegan alternatives, and even exploring flavorful regional variations, get ready to discover an array of gravies that will elevate your biscuits to a whole new level of deliciousness.

3.1 Traditional Sausage Gravy

A staple in southern cooking, traditional sausage gravy is a creamy, savory delight that perfectly complements fluffy biscuits. The combination of crumbled sausage, rich pan drippings, and milk creates a luscious, flavorful sauce that's hard to resist. Let's explore how to make this classic sausage gravy step by step:

Ingredients:

- 1/2 pound ground breakfast sausage (pork or turkey)
- 2 tablespoons all-purpose flour
- 2 cups whole milk
- Salt and freshly ground black pepper to taste

Instructions:

1. In a large skillet over medium heat, cook the breakfast sausage, breaking it apart into crumbles with a spoon, until it's browned and cooked through.
2. Sprinkle the flour over the cooked sausage and stir, allowing the flour to absorb the fat and coat the sausage evenly.
3. Gradually pour in the milk, stirring constantly to prevent lumps from forming. Cook the gravy until it thickens to your

desired consistency.

4. Season with salt and freshly ground black pepper to taste.

5. Pour this delicious sausage gravy generously over warm biscuits and enjoy the comforting flavors that epitomize biscuits and gravy at its finest.

3.2 Vegetarian and Vegan Gravy Alternatives

For those seeking meatless options or catering to vegan diets, we have flavorful alternatives that capture the essence of traditional gravy without compromising on taste. Let's explore two mouthwatering options:

a. Vegetarian Mushroom Gravy:
Ingredients:

- 2 tablespoons butter or olive oil
- 1 cup sliced mushrooms (cremini or button mushrooms work well)
- 2 tablespoons all-purpose flour
- 1 1/2 cups vegetable broth
- 1 cup whole milk or unsweetened plant-based milk
- Salt and freshly ground black pepper to taste

Instructions:

1. In a skillet over medium heat, melt the butter or heat the olive oil. Add the sliced mushrooms and sauté until they are tender and lightly browned.

2. Sprinkle the flour over the mushrooms and stir, allowing the flour to coat the mushrooms and cook for a minute.

3. Gradually pour in the vegetable broth and milk, stirring constantly to prevent lumps. Cook the gravy until it thickens to your desired consistency.

4. Season with salt and freshly ground black pepper to taste.

b. Vegan Cashew Gravy:
Ingredients:

- 1 cup raw cashews, soaked in water for at least 2 hours or overnight
- 1 1/2 cups vegetable broth
- 1/2 cup unsweetened plant-based milk (such as almond or soy)
- 1 tablespoon nutritional yeast (optional, for added flavor)
- 1 tablespoon soy sauce or tamari
- 1/2 teaspoon onion powder
- 1/2 teaspoon garlic powder
- Salt and freshly ground black pepper to taste

Instructions:

1. Drain and rinse the soaked cashews. In a blender, combine the soaked cashews, vegetable broth, plant-based milk, nutritional yeast, soy sauce, onion powder, and garlic powder. Blend until smooth and creamy.
2. Pour the mixture into a saucepan and heat over medium-low heat, stirring frequently until it thickens to your desired consistency.
3. Season with salt and freshly ground black pepper to taste.

Both of these alternatives offer a rich, savory gravy that pairs beautifully with biscuits and caters to a variety of dietary preferences.

3.3 Flavorful Regional Variations

Gravy comes in a delightful array of regional variations, each offering its own unique twist to the classic. Let's explore some of the most mouthwatering flavorful variations from around the world:

a. Red-Eye Gravy (Appalachian Region):

A distinctively tangy and smoky gravy made by deglazing the pan used to cook country ham with black coffee. It's a delightful regional specialty that's sure to tantalize your taste buds.

b. Biscuits and Chocolate Gravy (Ozark Region):

In the Ozarks, biscuits are often served with a sweet and indulgent chocolate gravy made from cocoa powder, sugar, milk, and a hint of butter. This unique sweet variation is a true treat for those with a sweet tooth.

c. Indian Biscuits and Gravy:

In India, biscuits and gravy take on an aromatic twist with spiced gravies featuring flavors like curry, turmeric, cumin, and coriander. This fusion of Indian and Western cuisines creates an exciting and flavorful pairing.

d. British Scones with Clotted Cream and Jam:

Across the pond, British scones serve as a cousin to American biscuits. These flaky delights are traditionally enjoyed with clotted cream and strawberry jam, offering a delightful twist on the classic biscuits and gravy experience.

As we explore these flavorful regional variations, you'll discover the endless possibilities that biscuits and gravy can offer. From classic to creative, traditional to inventive, gravies are the key to making each biscuit uniquely delicious. With this plethora of options, you can create your perfect biscuits and gravy combination, satisfying your taste buds and inspiring your culinary imagination.

So, whether you prefer the comforting embrace of traditional sausage gravy or the adventure of exploring regional flavors, there's a biscuit and gravy combination waiting for you to savor in this chapter of "Biscuits and Gravy Cookbook."

Chapter 4: Biscuit Sandwiches

In this chapter, we're taking biscuits to the next level by turning them into delectable and satisfying sandwiches. Whether you're craving a classic breakfast sandwich, a hearty Southern favorite, or a lighter veggie option, we've got the perfect biscuit sandwich recipes to delight your taste buds.

4.1 Classic Sausage and Egg Biscuit

This timeless breakfast combination is a crowd-pleaser for a reason. The marriage of savory sausage, perfectly cooked eggs, and a fluffy biscuit is the ultimate morning indulgence. Let's walk through how to create this beloved classic:

Ingredients:

- 4 classic buttermilk biscuits (from Chapter 2)
- 4 cooked sausage patties or links
- 4 large eggs
- 4 slices of cheddar cheese (optional)
- Salt and freshly ground black pepper to taste

Instructions:

1. Prepare the classic buttermilk biscuits following the instructions from Chapter 2.
2. Cook the sausage patties or links according to package instructions until they are golden brown and cooked through.
3. In a non-stick skillet over medium heat, cook the eggs sunny-side-up or to your desired doneness. Season with salt and freshly ground black pepper.
4. Slice the biscuits in half horizontally. Place a cooked sausage

patty on the bottom half of each biscuit, followed by a slice of cheddar cheese if desired.

5. Top the cheese with a sunny-side-up egg, and finally, place the top half of the biscuit on the egg.

These classic sausage and egg biscuits are the perfect way to kickstart your day with a hearty and satisfying breakfast.

4.2 Southern Fried Chicken Biscuit

A staple of Southern cuisine, the fried chicken biscuit sandwich combines the goodness of crispy, seasoned fried chicken with a tender biscuit. It's a delightful fusion of flavors and textures that's simply irresistible.

Ingredients:

- 4 classic buttermilk biscuits (from Chapter 2)
- 2 boneless, skinless chicken breasts, pounded to an even thickness
- 1 cup all-purpose flour
- 1 teaspoon paprika
- 1/2 teaspoon garlic powder
- 1/2 teaspoon onion powder
- 1/2 teaspoon dried thyme
- Salt and freshly ground black pepper to taste
- 1 cup buttermilk
- Vegetable oil for frying
- Pickles and hot sauce (optional, for serving)

Instructions:

1. Prepare the classic buttermilk biscuits following the instructions from Chapter 2.
2. In a shallow dish, whisk together the flour, paprika, garlic powder, onion powder, dried thyme, salt, and freshly ground

black pepper.

3. Dip each chicken breast into the buttermilk, then coat them evenly with the seasoned flour mixture, pressing the flour onto the chicken to adhere.

4. In a large skillet, heat about 1 inch of vegetable oil over medium-high heat until it reaches 350°F (175°C). Carefully add the coated chicken breasts to the hot oil and fry them for about 5-6 minutes per side or until they are golden brown and cooked through.

5. Transfer the fried chicken to a paper towel-lined plate to drain any excess oil.

6. Slice the biscuits in half horizontally. Place a fried chicken breast on the bottom half of each biscuit.

7. Serve the chicken biscuits as is, or add pickles and a dash of hot sauce for an extra kick.

The Southern fried chicken biscuit is a true indulgence that brings together the beloved flavors of the South in one scrumptious sandwich.

4.3 Veggie and Cheese Biscuit Sliders

For a lighter yet equally flavorful option, these veggie and cheese biscuit sliders are perfect for any time of the day. Packed with fresh vegetables, melted cheese, and small-sized biscuits, these sliders are a delightful addition to brunches, parties, or even as a snack.

Ingredients:

- 12 mini classic buttermilk biscuits (from Chapter 2)
- 1 large tomato, thinly sliced
- 1 avocado, sliced
- 1 cup baby spinach or arugula
- 4 slices of your favorite cheese (cheddar, Swiss, etc.)
- Mayonnaise or your preferred sauce (optional)

Instructions:

1. Prepare the mini classic buttermilk biscuits following the instructions from Chapter 2.
2. Slice each mini biscuit in half horizontally.
3. Build the sliders by layering a slice of tomato, a few avocado slices, and a handful of baby spinach or arugula on the bottom half of each biscuit.
4. Top the vegetables with a slice of cheese, and optionally, spread a thin layer of mayonnaise or your preferred sauce on the top half of the biscuit.
5. Place the top half of the biscuit on the cheese to complete the sliders.

These veggie and cheese biscuit sliders offer a fresh and delightful alternative to traditional meat-filled sandwiches, making them a perfect addition to any gathering or a quick and satisfying snack.

With these biscuit sandwiches in your culinary repertoire, you can enjoy biscuits beyond breakfast and elevate your meals with delicious and creative combinations. From classic sausage and egg to indulgent fried chicken, and even lighter veggie sliders, these biscuit sandwiches are sure to please and leave everyone craving more. So, let's dive into the world of biscuits and explore their endless potential as sandwich delights!

Chapter 5: Biscuits with a Twist

In this chapter, we're pushing the boundaries of biscuit creativity by exploring unconventional yet utterly delicious ways to enjoy biscuits. From a hearty breakfast casserole to transforming biscuits into delightful waffles and pancakes, and even incorporating them into a savory pot pie, get ready to experience biscuits like never before!

5.1 Biscuit Breakfast Casserole

This comforting and satisfying biscuit breakfast casserole is the perfect way to start your day. Packed with flavorful ingredients and topped with fluffy biscuits, it's a crowd-pleasing dish that's ideal for family brunches or lazy weekend mornings.

Ingredients:

- 1 pound breakfast sausage (pork or turkey), cooked and crumbled
- 1 cup diced bell peppers (red, green, or a mix)
- 1 cup diced onions
- 1 cup diced tomatoes
- 1 cup shredded cheddar cheese
- 6 large eggs
- 1/2 cup milk
- 1 teaspoon dried thyme
- Salt and freshly ground black pepper to taste
- 1 tube of refrigerated biscuits (8 biscuits)

Instructions:

1. Preheat your oven to 375°F (190°C) and grease a 9x13-inch baking dish.

2. In a large skillet over medium heat, cook the breakfast sausage until it's browned and cooked through. Remove the sausage from the skillet and set it aside.
3. In the same skillet, sauté the diced bell peppers and onions until they are tender and lightly browned.
4. In a large mixing bowl, whisk together the eggs, milk, dried thyme, salt, and freshly ground black pepper.
5. Add the cooked breakfast sausage, sautéed bell peppers and onions, diced tomatoes, and shredded cheddar cheese to the egg mixture. Stir until all the ingredients are well combined.
6. Pour the mixture into the greased baking dish.
7. Cut the refrigerated biscuits into quarters and scatter them evenly on top of the egg mixture.
8. Bake the casserole in the preheated oven for 25-30 minutes or until the biscuits are golden brown and the eggs are set.
9. Allow the casserole to cool slightly before serving.

This biscuit breakfast casserole is a delightful medley of flavors and textures, making it a perfect centerpiece for a hearty and memorable breakfast or brunch.

5.2 Biscuit Waffles and Pancakes

Take your breakfast game to the next level by transforming classic biscuits into delightful waffles and pancakes. These fluffy creations bring together the best of both worlds—the taste of biscuits and the texture of waffles or pancakes.

Biscuit Waffles:

Ingredients:

- 1 batch of classic buttermilk biscuit dough (from Chapter 2)
- Cooking spray or melted butter for greasing the waffle iron

Instructions:

1. Preheat your waffle iron according to the manufacturer's instructions.
2. Prepare the classic buttermilk biscuit dough following the instructions from Chapter 2.
3. Lightly grease the preheated waffle iron with cooking spray or melted butter.
4. Place a portion of biscuit dough onto the waffle iron, making sure not to overcrowd it.
5. Close the waffle iron and cook the biscuit waffles according to the manufacturer's instructions until they are golden brown and cooked through.
6. Serve the biscuit waffles warm with your favorite toppings, such as butter, maple syrup, honey, or fruit.

Biscuit Pancakes:

Ingredients:

- 1 batch of classic buttermilk biscuit dough (from Chapter 2)
- Cooking spray or melted butter for greasing the griddle or

skillet

Instructions:

1. Preheat a griddle or skillet over medium heat.
2. Prepare the classic buttermilk biscuit dough following the instructions from Chapter 2.
3. Lightly grease the griddle or skillet with cooking spray or melted butter.
4. Drop spoonfuls of biscuit dough onto the griddle or skillet to form pancakes.
5. Cook the biscuit pancakes for 2-3 minutes on each side or until they are golden brown and cooked through.
6. Serve the biscuit pancakes warm with your favorite pancake toppings, such as syrup, jam, fresh berries, or whipped cream.

Biscuit waffles and pancakes offer a delightful twist on traditional breakfast fare, bringing a touch of biscuit goodness to the beloved classics.

5.3 Biscuit and Gravy Pot Pie

In this creative and hearty dish, we're combining the best of both worlds—biscuits and gravy—in a savory pot pie that's sure to become a family favorite. This warm and comforting pot pie is the ultimate comfort food for chilly evenings or lazy weekends.

Ingredients:

- 1 pound ground sausage (pork or turkey)
- 1/4 cup unsalted butter
- 1/4 cup all-purpose flour
- 2 cups chicken or vegetable broth
- 1 cup milk
- Salt and freshly ground black pepper to taste
- 1 batch of classic buttermilk biscuit dough (from Chapter 2)

Instructions:

1. Preheat your oven to 375°F (190°C).
2. In a large skillet over medium heat, cook the ground sausage until it's browned and cooked through. Remove the sausage from the skillet and set it aside.
3. In the same skillet, melt the unsalted butter over medium heat. Stir in the all-purpose flour to create a roux, and cook for a couple of minutes to eliminate the raw flour taste.
4. Gradually pour in the chicken or vegetable broth and milk, stirring constantly to prevent lumps. Cook the gravy until it thickens to your desired consistency.
5. Add the cooked sausage to the gravy and season with salt and freshly ground black pepper to taste. Stir until all the ingredients are well combined.
6. Pour the sausage and gravy mixture into a greased 9x13-inch baking dish.
7. Prepare the classic buttermilk biscuit dough following the instructions from Chapter 2. Drop spoonfuls of biscuit dough onto the top of the sausage and gravy mixture, creating a biscuit topping.
8. Bake the pot pie in the preheated oven for 20-25 minutes or until the biscuits are golden brown and cooked through.

This biscuit and gravy pot pie is a savory delight that combines the comforting flavors of biscuits and gravy with the heartiness of a classic pot pie.

With these creative biscuit twists, you'll be able to enjoy biscuits in exciting new ways, from a satisfying breakfast casserole to fluffy biscuit waffles and pancakes, and even a savory biscuit and gravy pot pie.

Chapter 6: International Biscuit Delights

In this chapter, we embark on a culinary journey across the globe to discover delightful biscuit variations from different countries. From the elegant British scones served with clotted cream to the aromatic Indian biscuits with spiced gravy, and the rustic Australian "damper" bread with bush gravy, prepare to be enchanted by the unique flavors and traditions that international biscuits bring to the table.

6.1 British Scones with Clotted Cream

The quintessential British scone, with its delicate crumb and buttery goodness, is a beloved treat served with afternoon tea or as a delightful breakfast option. Paired with luxurious clotted cream and sweet strawberry jam, it's a delightful indulgence that perfectly captures the essence of British teatime.

Ingredients:

- 2 cups all-purpose flour
- 1/4 cup granulated sugar
- 1 tablespoon baking powder
- 1/2 teaspoon salt
- 1/3 cup cold unsalted butter, cut into small cubes
- 2/3 cup whole milk
- Clotted cream and strawberry jam (or your favorite preserves) for serving

Instructions:

Preheat your oven to 425°F (220°C) and line a baking sheet with parchment paper.

1. In a large mixing bowl, whisk together the flour, sugar, baking

powder, and salt.

2. Add the cold butter cubes to the dry ingredients and use a pastry cutter or your fingertips to work the butter into the flour until the mixture resembles coarse crumbs.

3. Gradually pour in the whole milk, stirring with a fork until the dough just comes together.

4. Turn the dough out onto a lightly floured surface and gently knead it a few times until it forms a cohesive ball.

5. Pat the dough into a circle about 3/4-inch thick. Use a biscuit cutter or a glass to cut out scones, and place them on the prepared baking sheet.

6. Bake the scones for 12 to 15 minutes or until they are golden brown on top.

7. Serve the warm scones with clotted cream and strawberry jam for a delightful British teatime experience.

The British scones with clotted cream are a delightful reminder of English traditions and the perfect treat to enjoy with a cup of tea or coffee.

6.2 Indian Biscuits with Spiced Gravy

In India, biscuits take on an aromatic twist with spiced gravies featuring flavors like curry, turmeric, cumin, and coriander. This fusion of Indian and Western cuisines creates an exciting and flavorful pairing that's sure to intrigue your taste buds.

Ingredients for Biscuits:

- 2 cups all-purpose flour
- 1 tablespoon baking powder
- 1/2 teaspoon baking soda
- 1 teaspoon salt
- 6 tablespoons cold unsalted butter, cut into small cubes
- 1 cup buttermilk

Instructions for Biscuits:

Preheat your oven to 450°F (230°C) and line a baking sheet with parchment paper.

1. In a large mixing bowl, whisk together the flour, baking powder, baking soda, and salt.
2. Add the cold butter cubes to the dry ingredients and use a pastry cutter or your fingertips to work the butter into the flour until the mixture resembles coarse crumbs.
3. Gradually pour in the buttermilk, stirring with a fork until the dough just comes together.
4. Turn the dough out onto a lightly floured surface and gently knead it a few times until it forms a cohesive ball.
5. Pat the dough into a circle about 3/4-inch thick. Use a biscuit cutter or a glass to cut out biscuits, and place them on the prepared baking sheet.
6. Bake the biscuits for 12 to 15 minutes or until they are golden brown on top.

Ingredients for Spiced Gravy:

- 2 tablespoons vegetable oil
- 1 onion, finely chopped
- 2 cloves garlic, minced
- 1-inch piece of ginger, grated
- 1 tablespoon curry powder
- 1/2 teaspoon ground turmeric
- 1/2 teaspoon ground cumin
- 1/2 teaspoon ground coriander
- 1/4 teaspoon cayenne pepper (optional, for heat)
- 1 cup vegetable broth
- 1 cup coconut milk
- Salt and freshly ground black pepper to taste

Instructions for Spiced Gravy:

1. In a skillet over medium heat, heat the vegetable oil. Add the chopped onion and sauté until it's translucent.
2. Stir in the minced garlic and grated ginger, and cook for another minute until the mixture becomes fragrant.
3. Add the curry powder, turmeric, cumin, coriander, and cayenne pepper (if using). Stir to coat the onions, garlic, and ginger with the spices.
4. Pour in the vegetable broth and coconut milk, and bring the mixture to a simmer. Cook until the gravy thickens and the flavors meld together, about 5 minutes.
5. Season the spiced gravy with salt and freshly ground black pepper to taste.
6. Serve the Indian biscuits warm with the aromatic spiced gravy, and experience the delightful fusion of Indian and Western flavors.

6.3 Australian "Damper" Bread with Bush Gravy

In the Australian outback, "damper" bread is a rustic and traditional bread baked over an open fire. Paired with hearty "bush gravy," this humble yet flavorful combination is a testament to Australian bush cooking.

Ingredients for Damper Bread:

- 4 cups self-rising flour
- Pinch of salt
- 1 1/2 cups water

Instructions for Damper Bread:

1. In a large mixing bowl, whisk together the self-rising flour and a pinch of salt.
2. Gradually add water, stirring with a spoon until the mixture comes together into a dough.
3. Turn the dough out onto a floured surface and shape it into a round loaf.
4. Place the loaf on a lightly greased baking sheet and use a knife to make a cross on the top.
5. Bake the damper bread in a preheated oven at 375°F (190°C) for 45 to 50 minutes or until it sounds hollow when tapped on the bottom.

Ingredients for Bush Gravy:

- 2 tablespoons vegetable oil
- 1 onion, finely chopped
- 1 carrot, finely diced
- 1 celery stalk, finely diced
- 2 tablespoons all-purpose flour

- 2 cups beef or vegetable broth
- Salt and freshly ground black pepper to taste

Instructions for Bush Gravy:

1. In a skillet over medium heat, heat the vegetable oil. Add the chopped onion, carrot, and celery, and sauté until they are tender.
2. Stir in the all-purpose flour to create a roux, and cook for a couple of minutes to eliminate the raw flour taste.
3. Gradually pour in the beef or vegetable broth, stirring constantly to prevent lumps. Cook the gravy until it thickens to your desired consistency.
4. Season the bush gravy with salt and freshly ground black pepper to taste.
5. Serve slices of the Australian damper bread warm with the hearty bush gravy, and experience the rustic charm of Australian bush cooking.

In this chapter, we've explored international biscuit delights that take us on a flavorful journey around the world. From the elegance of British scones with clotted cream to the aromatic Indian biscuits with spiced gravy, and the rustic charm of Australian damper bread with bush gravy, these international variations showcase the versatility and adaptability of biscuits in diverse culinary traditions.

Chapter 7: Sweet Biscuit Treats

In this chapter, we're indulging our sweet tooth with a delightful array of biscuit treats that are perfect for dessert, brunch, or any time you crave something sweet. From the luscious honey butter biscuits to the berry-filled delights with glaze, and the irresistible cinnamon sugar biscuit bites, get ready to experience the sweeter side of biscuits!

7.1 Honey Butter Biscuits

These honey butter biscuits are a heavenly treat that combines the natural sweetness of honey with the rich creaminess of butter. Whether enjoyed warm from the oven or with a drizzle of honey, they are an irresistible delight that's perfect for any occasion.

Ingredients:

- 2 cups all-purpose flour
- 1 tablespoon baking powder
- 1/2 teaspoon baking soda
- 1 teaspoon salt
- 6 tablespoons cold unsalted butter, cut into small cubes
- 1/3 cup honey
- 2/3 cup buttermilk

Instructions:

1. Preheat your oven to 450°F (230°C) and line a baking sheet with parchment paper.
2. In a large mixing bowl, whisk together the flour, baking powder, baking soda, and salt.
3. Add the cold butter cubes to the dry ingredients and use a pastry cutter or your fingertips to work the butter into the

flour until the mixture resembles coarse crumbs.

4. In a separate bowl, whisk together the honey and buttermilk until well combined.
5. Gradually pour the honey and buttermilk mixture into the dry ingredients, stirring with a fork until the dough just comes together.
6. Turn the dough out onto a lightly floured surface and gently knead it a few times until it forms a cohesive ball.
7. Pat the dough into a circle about 3/4-inch thick. Use a biscuit cutter or a glass to cut out biscuits, and place them on the prepared baking sheet.
8. Bake the biscuits for 12 to 15 minutes or until they are golden brown on top.
9. Serve the honey butter biscuits warm, and optionally drizzle with a little extra honey for an extra touch of sweetness.

These honey butter biscuits are a delightful combination of buttery goodness and natural sweetness, making them a crowd-pleasing treat for any sweet occasion.

7.2 Berry-Filled Biscuits with Glaze

These berry-filled biscuits are a burst of fruity goodness, filled with your favorite berries and topped with a luscious glaze. They're a wonderful way to enjoy the vibrant flavors of fresh berries in a delightful biscuit form.

Ingredients for Biscuits:

- 2 cups all-purpose flour
- 1 tablespoon baking powder
- 1/2 teaspoon baking soda
- 1 teaspoon salt
- 6 tablespoons cold unsalted butter, cut into small cubes
- 2/3 cup buttermilk
- 1 cup fresh berries (strawberries, blueberries, raspberries, or a mix)

Instructions for Biscuits:

1. Preheat your oven to 450°F (230°C) and line a baking sheet with parchment paper.
2. In a large mixing bowl, whisk together the flour, baking powder, baking soda, and salt.
3. Add the cold butter cubes to the dry ingredients and use a pastry cutter or your fingertips to work the butter into the flour until the mixture resembles coarse crumbs.
4. Gradually pour in the buttermilk, stirring with a fork until the dough just comes together.
5. Turn the dough out onto a lightly floured surface and gently knead it a few times until it forms a cohesive ball.
6. Pat the dough into a circle about 3/4-inch thick. Use a biscuit cutter or a glass to cut out biscuits, and place them on the prepared baking sheet.
7. Press an indentation in the center of each biscuit with your

thumb or the back of a spoon to create a space for the berries.

8. Fill each indentation with a mixture of fresh berries.

Ingredients for Glaze:

- 1 cup powdered sugar
- 2 tablespoons milk
- 1/2 teaspoon vanilla extract

Instructions for Glaze:

1. In a small bowl, whisk together the powdered sugar, milk, and vanilla extract until the glaze is smooth and well combined.
2. Drizzle the glaze over the berry-filled biscuits.

These berry-filled biscuits with glaze are a delightful explosion of fruity sweetness, making them a delightful treat for brunch, dessert, or any time you crave something sweet and refreshing.

7.3 Cinnamon Sugar Biscuit Bites

For a delightful bite-sized treat that's easy to make and impossible to resist, these cinnamon sugar biscuit bites are a true delight. With their warm cinnamon flavor and a touch of sweetness, they're a perfect treat for sharing with family and friends.

Ingredients:

- 1 batch of classic buttermilk biscuit dough (from Chapter 2)
- 1/2 cup granulated sugar
- 1 tablespoon ground cinnamon
- 4 tablespoons unsalted butter, melted

Instructions:

1. Preheat your oven to 450°F (230°C) and line a baking sheet with parchment paper.
2. Prepare the classic buttermilk biscuit dough following the instructions from Chapter 2.
3. In a shallow dish, whisk together the granulated sugar and ground cinnamon to make the cinnamon sugar mixture.
4. Pinch off small pieces of biscuit dough and roll them into bite-sized balls.
5. Dip each biscuit ball into the melted butter, making sure it's well coated.
6. Roll the butter-coated biscuit ball in the cinnamon sugar mixture until it's fully coated.
7. Place the coated biscuit balls on the prepared baking sheet, leaving some space between them.
8. Bake the cinnamon sugar biscuit bites for 10 to 12 minutes or until they are golden brown and cooked through.

These irresistible cinnamon sugar biscuit bites are a delightful treat to enjoy warm from the oven, making them a perfect sweet indulgence for any occasion.

In this chapter, we've explored a delightful array of sweet biscuit treats that bring a touch of sweetness to your table. From the luscious honey butter biscuits to the berry-filled delights with glaze, and the irresistible cinnamon sugar biscuit bites, these treats are perfect for dessert, brunch, or any time you crave something sweet.

Chapter 8: Savory Gravy Creations

In this chapter, we're diving into the world of savory gravies that elevate biscuits to new heights of deliciousness. From the rich and earthy mushroom and onion gravy to the indulgent bacon and shallot gravy, and the vibrant roasted red pepper gravy, get ready to savor the enticing flavors that savory gravies bring to the biscuit experience.

8.1 Mushroom and Onion Gravy

This savory mushroom and onion gravy is a delightful combination of earthy mushrooms, sweet caramelized onions, and rich, flavorful gravy. It's a vegetarian-friendly option that adds a touch of sophistication to any biscuit dish.

Ingredients:

- 2 tablespoons unsalted butter
- 1 large onion, thinly sliced
- 8 ounces mushrooms (cremini, button, or a mix), sliced
- 2 tablespoons all-purpose flour
- 2 cups vegetable broth
- 1/2 cup heavy cream (or substitute with whole milk for a lighter version)
- Salt and freshly ground black pepper to taste
- Fresh thyme leaves for garnish (optional)

Instructions:

1. In a large skillet over medium heat, melt the unsalted butter. Add the thinly sliced onion and sauté until they become soft and caramelized, about 10-15 minutes.
2. Add the sliced mushrooms to the skillet and cook until they

are tender and browned, about 5-7 minutes.

3. Sprinkle the all-purpose flour over the mushrooms and onions, stirring to coat them evenly.
4. Gradually pour in the vegetable broth, stirring constantly to prevent lumps from forming.
5. Bring the mixture to a simmer and cook until the gravy thickens, about 5 minutes.
6. Stir in the heavy cream (or whole milk) and let the gravy simmer for an additional 2-3 minutes until it reaches your desired consistency.
7. Season the mushroom and onion gravy with salt and freshly ground black pepper to taste.
8. Serve this rich and flavorful gravy generously over warm biscuits and garnish with fresh thyme leaves if desired.

This mushroom and onion gravy is a delightful way to enjoy the savory goodness of mushrooms and onions, making it a perfect companion for biscuits in any savory meal.

8.2 Bacon and Shallot Gravy

For an indulgent and savory gravy option, this bacon and shallot gravy delivers bold flavors that will delight your taste buds. The combination of smoky bacon and sweet shallots creates a heavenly sauce that pairs perfectly with biscuits.

Ingredients:

- 4 slices bacon, chopped
- 2 large shallots, finely chopped
- 2 tablespoons all-purpose flour
- 2 cups chicken or vegetable broth
- 1/2 cup heavy cream (or substitute with whole milk for a lighter version)
- Salt and freshly ground black pepper to taste
- Fresh parsley for garnish (optional)

Instructions:

1. In a large skillet over medium heat, cook the chopped bacon until it becomes crispy. Remove the bacon from the skillet, leaving the bacon drippings in the pan.
2. Add the finely chopped shallots to the skillet and sauté them in the bacon drippings until they are soft and translucent.
3. Sprinkle the all-purpose flour over the shallots, stirring to coat them evenly.
4. Gradually pour in the chicken or vegetable broth, stirring constantly to prevent lumps from forming.
5. Bring the mixture to a simmer and cook until the gravy thickens, about 5 minutes.
6. Stir in the heavy cream (or whole milk) and let the gravy simmer for an additional 2-3 minutes until it reaches your desired consistency.
7. Season the bacon and shallot gravy with salt and freshly

ground black pepper to taste.

8. Stir in the cooked bacon pieces and mix well.
9. Serve this indulgent bacon and shallot gravy generously over warm biscuits and garnish with fresh parsley if desired.

This bacon and shallot gravy is a delectable treat that combines the smoky goodness of bacon with the sweetness of shallots, creating a gravy that's sure to impress and satisfy your cravings.

8.3 Roasted Red Pepper Gravy

For a burst of vibrant flavor, this roasted red pepper gravy is a unique and delightful choice. The roasted red peppers add a sweet and tangy twist to the classic gravy, making it a truly memorable addition to any biscuit dish.

Ingredients:

- 2 large red bell peppers
- 2 tablespoons olive oil
- 1 small onion, finely chopped
- 2 tablespoons all-purpose flour
- 2 cups vegetable or chicken broth
- 1/2 cup heavy cream (or substitute with whole milk for a lighter version)
- Salt and freshly ground black pepper to taste
- Fresh basil leaves for garnish (optional)

Instructions:

1. Preheat your oven to 450°F (230°C).
2. Cut the red bell peppers in half and remove the seeds and membranes.
3. Place the pepper halves on a baking sheet, skin side up. Drizzle the olive oil over the peppers.

4. Roast the red bell peppers in the preheated oven for 20-25 minutes or until the skins become charred and blistered.

5. Remove the peppers from the oven and let them cool slightly. Once cooled, peel off the charred skins and chop the roasted red peppers.

6. In a large skillet, sauté the finely chopped onion until it becomes soft and translucent.

7. Add the chopped roasted red peppers to the skillet and cook for a few minutes to blend the flavors.

8. Sprinkle the all-purpose flour over the peppers and onions, stirring to coat them evenly.

9. Gradually pour in the vegetable or chicken broth, stirring constantly to prevent lumps from forming.

10. Bring the mixture to a simmer and cook until the gravy thickens, about 5 minutes.

11. Stir in the heavy cream (or whole milk) and let the gravy simmer for an additional 2-3 minutes until it reaches your desired consistency.

12. Season the roasted red pepper gravy with salt and freshly ground black pepper to taste.

13. Serve this vibrant and flavorful gravy generously over warm biscuits and garnish with fresh basil leaves if desired.

This roasted red pepper gravy is a delightful explosion of flavors, adding a touch of brightness and sweetness to your biscuit creations and making them a standout savory treat.

In this chapter, we've explored a delightful array of savory gravy creations that bring a world of flavors to your biscuit experience. From the rich and earthy mushroom and onion gravy to the indulgent bacon and shallot gravy, and the vibrant roasted red pepper gravy, these savory gravies elevate biscuits to new heights of deliciousness.

Chapter 9: Biscuit Breakfast Bowls

In this chapter, we're crafting hearty and flavorful breakfast bowls that feature biscuits as the star ingredient. From the classic biscuits and sausage gravy bowl to the elegant Biscuit Benedict with poached eggs, and the wholesome veggie-loaded biscuit bowl, these breakfast creations are sure to kick-start your day with a delicious and satisfying meal.

9.1 Biscuits and Sausage Gravy Bowl

A quintessential Southern breakfast favorite, this biscuits and sausage gravy bowl combines fluffy biscuits smothered in rich sausage gravy. It's a comforting and indulgent dish that brings a taste of Southern hospitality to your breakfast table.

Ingredients for Biscuits:

- 2 cups all-purpose flour
- 1 tablespoon baking powder
- 1/2 teaspoon baking soda
- 1 teaspoon salt
- 6 tablespoons cold unsalted butter, cut into small cubes
- 2/3 cup buttermilk

Instructions for Biscuits:

1. Preheat your oven to 450°F (230°C) and line a baking sheet with parchment paper.
2. In a large mixing bowl, whisk together the flour, baking powder, baking soda, and salt.
3. Add the cold butter cubes to the dry ingredients and use a

pastry cutter or your fingertips to work the butter into the flour until the mixture resembles coarse crumbs.

4. Gradually pour in the buttermilk, stirring with a fork until the dough just comes together.

5. Turn the dough out onto a lightly floured surface and gently knead it a few times until it forms a cohesive ball.

6. Pat the dough into a circle about 3/4-inch thick. Use a biscuit cutter or a glass to cut out biscuits, and place them on the prepared baking sheet.

7. Bake the biscuits for 12 to 15 minutes or until they are golden brown on top.

Ingredients for Sausage Gravy:

- 1 pound ground sausage (pork or turkey)
- 1/4 cup unsalted butter
- 1/4 cup all-purpose flour
- 2 cups whole milk
- Salt and freshly ground black pepper to taste

Instructions for Sausage Gravy:

1. In a large skillet over medium heat, cook the ground sausage until it's browned and cooked through. Remove the sausage from the skillet and set it aside.

2. In the same skillet, melt the unsalted butter over medium heat. Stir in the all-purpose flour to create a roux, and cook for a couple of minutes to eliminate the raw flour taste.

3. Gradually pour in the whole milk, stirring constantly to prevent lumps. Cook the gravy until it thickens to your desired consistency.

4. Add the cooked sausage to the gravy and season with salt and freshly ground black pepper to taste. Stir until all the

ingredients are well combined.

Assemble the Biscuits and Sausage Gravy Bowl:

- Split the freshly baked biscuits in half and place them at the bottom of a serving bowl.
- Ladle a generous amount of the sausage gravy over the biscuits.
- Optionally, garnish with a sprinkle of freshly ground black pepper or chopped fresh parsley.
- Serve the biscuits and sausage gravy bowl while warm and enjoy the comforting flavors of the South.

9.2 Biscuit Benedict with Poached Eggs

This elegant and gourmet Biscuit Benedict puts a delightful twist on the classic Eggs Benedict by swapping the English muffins with fluffy biscuits. Topped with poached eggs and velvety hollandaise sauce, it's a breakfast indulgence fit for special occasions or leisurely brunches.

Ingredients for Biscuits:

- 2 cups all-purpose flour
- 1 tablespoon baking powder
- 1/2 teaspoon baking soda
- 1 teaspoon salt
- 6 tablespoons cold unsalted butter, cut into small cubes
- 2/3 cup buttermilk

Instructions for Biscuits:

1. Preheat your oven to 450°F (230°C) and line a baking sheet with parchment paper.
2. In a large mixing bowl, whisk together the flour, baking powder, baking soda, and salt.
3. Add the cold butter cubes to the dry ingredients and use a pastry cutter or your fingertips to work the butter into the flour until the mixture resembles coarse crumbs.
4. Gradually pour in the buttermilk, stirring with a fork until the dough just comes together.
5. Turn the dough out onto a lightly floured surface and gently knead it a few times until it forms a cohesive ball.
6. Pat the dough into a circle about 3/4-inch thick. Use a biscuit cutter or a glass to cut out biscuits, and place them on the prepared baking sheet.
7. Bake the biscuits for 12 to 15 minutes or until they are golden brown on top.

Ingredients for Poached Eggs and Hollandaise Sauce:

- 4 large eggs
- 1 tablespoon white vinegar
- 1/2 cup (1 stick) unsalted butter, melted
- 3 large egg yolks
- 1 tablespoon lemon juice
- Salt and freshly ground black pepper to taste
- Pinch of cayenne pepper (optional)

Instructions for Poached Eggs and Hollandaise Sauce:

1. Fill a large saucepan with about 2 inches of water and add the white vinegar. Bring the water to a gentle simmer over medium heat.
2. Crack each egg into a small bowl or ramekin, taking care not to break the yolks.
3. Carefully slide each egg into the simmering water, one at a time. Poach the eggs for about 3-4 minutes or until the whites are set, but the yolks are still runny.
4. Remove the poached eggs with a slotted spoon and place them on a plate lined with a paper towel to absorb any excess water.

For the Hollandaise Sauce:

1. In a heatproof bowl, whisk together the egg yolks and lemon juice until well combined.
2. Place the bowl over a pot of simmering water (double boiler) and whisk constantly until the mixture begins to thicken, about 2-3 minutes.
3. Slowly drizzle in the melted butter while continuing to whisk vigorously until the sauce is smooth and creamy.
4. Season the hollandaise sauce with salt, freshly ground black pepper, and a pinch of cayenne pepper if desired.

Assemble the Biscuit Benedict:

1. Split the freshly baked biscuits in half and place them on a serving plate.
2. Top each biscuit half with a poached egg.
3. Drizzle the velvety hollandaise sauce over the poached eggs.
4. Optionally, garnish with a sprinkle of freshly ground black pepper and a sprig of fresh dill or chives for a pop of color.
5. Serve the Biscuit Benedict while warm, and indulge in the decadent combination of poached eggs and hollandaise sauce on fluffy biscuits.

9.3 Veggie-Loaded Biscuit Bowl

For a wholesome and veggie-packed breakfast bowl, this veggie-loaded biscuit bowl is the way to go. Filled with nutritious vegetables and topped with your favorite savory additions, it's a delicious and satisfying way to start your day on a healthy note.

Ingredients for Biscuits:

- 2 cups all-purpose flour
- 1 tablespoon baking powder
- 1/2 teaspoon baking soda
- 1 teaspoon salt
- 6 tablespoons cold unsalted butter, cut into small cubes
- 2/3 cup buttermilk

Instructions for Biscuits:

1. Preheat your oven to 450°F (230°C) and line a baking sheet with parchment paper.
2. In a large mixing bowl, whisk together the flour, baking powder, baking soda, and salt.
3. Add the cold butter cubes to the dry ingredients and use a pastry cutter or your fingertips to work the butter into the flour until the mixture resembles coarse crumbs.
4. Gradually pour in the buttermilk, stirring with a fork until the dough just comes together.
5. Turn the dough out onto a lightly floured surface and gently knead it a few times until it forms a cohesive ball.
6. Pat the dough into a circle about 3/4-inch thick. Use a biscuit cutter or a glass to cut out biscuits, and place them on the prepared baking sheet.
7. Bake the biscuits for 12 to 15 minutes or until they are golden brown on top.

Ingredients for Veggie-Loaded Biscuit Bowl:

- 1 tablespoon olive oil
- 1 red bell pepper, diced
- 1 yellow bell pepper, diced
- 1 zucchini, diced
- 1 cup cherry tomatoes, halved
- 2 cups fresh spinach or baby kale
- Salt and freshly ground black pepper to taste
- Grated cheddar cheese for topping (optional)

Instructions for Veggie-Loaded Biscuit Bowl:

1. In a large skillet over medium heat, heat the olive oil. Add the diced red and yellow bell peppers, and sauté until they become tender.
2. Stir in the diced zucchini and halved cherry tomatoes, and continue to sauté until the vegetables are cooked but still have a slight crunch.
3. Add the fresh spinach or baby kale to the skillet, and sauté until the greens wilt down.
4. Season the vegetable mixture with salt and freshly ground black pepper to taste.

Assemble the Veggie-Loaded Biscuit Bowl:

1. Split the freshly baked biscuits in half and place them at the bottom of a serving bowl.
2. Spoon the sautéed vegetable mixture over the biscuits.
3. Optionally, sprinkle some grated cheddar cheese over the top for added richness and flavor.
4. Serve the veggie-loaded biscuit bowl while warm and enjoy a wholesome and satisfying breakfast that's packed with colorful vegetables.

In this chapter, we've crafted hearty and flavorful biscuit breakfast bowls that are perfect for starting your day with a delicious and satisfying meal. From the classic biscuits and sausage gravy bowl to the elegant Biscuit Benedict with poached eggs, and the wholesome veggie-loaded biscuit bowl, these breakfast creations celebrate the versatility of biscuits in a variety of savory and delectable combinations.

Chapter 10: Gourmet Biscuit Meals

In this chapter, we're venturing into the world of gourmet biscuit meals that elevate biscuits to a luxurious and indulgent experience. From the elegant lobster bisque served over biscuits to the succulent filet mignon with red wine gravy, and the delectable spinach and artichoke biscuits, these gourmet creations are perfect for special occasions or when you want to treat yourself to something extraordinary.

10.1 Lobster Bisque over Biscuits

This elegant dish combines the richness of lobster bisque with the comforting goodness of biscuits. The creamy bisque with tender chunks of lobster is a luxurious pairing with fluffy biscuits, creating a gourmet meal fit for a special celebration.

Ingredients for Biscuits:

- 2 cups all-purpose flour
- 1 tablespoon baking powder
- 1/2 teaspoon baking soda
- 1 teaspoon salt
- 6 tablespoons cold unsalted butter, cut into small cubes
- 2/3 cup buttermilk

Instructions for Biscuits:

1. Preheat your oven to 450°F (230°C) and line a baking sheet with parchment paper.
2. In a large mixing bowl, whisk together the flour, baking powder, baking soda, and salt.
3. Add the cold butter cubes to the dry ingredients and use a

pastry cutter or your fingertips to work the butter into the flour until the mixture resembles coarse crumbs.

4. Gradually pour in the buttermilk, stirring with a fork until the dough just comes together.
5. Turn the dough out onto a lightly floured surface and gently knead it a few times until it forms a cohesive ball.
6. Pat the dough into a circle about 3/4-inch thick. Use a biscuit cutter or a glass to cut out biscuits, and place them on the prepared baking sheet.
7. Bake the biscuits for 12 to 15 minutes or until they are golden brown on top.

Ingredients for Lobster Bisque:

- 2 lobster tails, shells removed and chopped into chunks
- 2 tablespoons unsalted butter
- 1/2 cup finely chopped onion
- 1/2 cup finely chopped carrot
- 1/2 cup finely chopped celery
- 2 cloves garlic, minced
- 2 tablespoons all-purpose flour
- 2 cups seafood or chicken broth
- 1 cup heavy cream
- Salt and freshly ground black pepper to taste
- Chopped fresh parsley for garnish (optional)

Instructions for Lobster Bisque:

1. In a large saucepan over medium heat, melt the unsalted butter. Add the chopped onion, carrot, and celery, and sauté until they are softened.
2. Stir in the minced garlic and cook for another minute until the mixture becomes fragrant.

3. Sprinkle the all-purpose flour over the vegetables, stirring to coat them evenly.
4. Gradually pour in the seafood or chicken broth, stirring constantly to prevent lumps.
5. Add the chopped lobster chunks to the saucepan and bring the mixture to a simmer. Cook for about 8-10 minutes or until the lobster is cooked through.
6. Stir in the heavy cream and let the bisque simmer for an additional 2-3 minutes until it reaches your desired consistency.
7. Season the lobster bisque with salt and freshly ground black pepper to taste.

Assemble the Lobster Bisque over Biscuits:

1. Split the freshly baked biscuits in half and place them at the bottom of a serving bowl.
2. Ladle a generous amount of the lobster bisque over the biscuits.
3. Optionally, garnish with chopped fresh parsley for a pop of color and added freshness.
4. Serve the Lobster Bisque over Biscuits while warm, and indulge in the luxurious flavors of tender lobster paired with fluffy biscuits.

10.2 Filet Mignon and Red Wine Gravy

For a truly decadent meal, this gourmet dish features tender filet mignon served with a rich red wine gravy. Paired with warm biscuits, it's a luxurious and flavorful combination that's sure to impress your guests or make any occasion extra special.

Ingredients for Biscuits:

- 2 cups all-purpose flour
- 1 tablespoon baking powder
- 1/2 teaspoon baking soda
- 1 teaspoon salt
- 6 tablespoons cold unsalted butter, cut into small cubes
- 2/3 cup buttermilk

Instructions for Biscuits:

1. Preheat your oven to 450°F (230°C) and line a baking sheet with parchment paper.
2. In a large mixing bowl, whisk together the flour, baking powder, baking soda, and salt.
3. Add the cold butter cubes to the dry ingredients and use a pastry cutter or your fingertips to work the butter into the flour until the mixture resembles coarse crumbs.
4. Gradually pour in the buttermilk, stirring with a fork until the dough just comes together.
5. Turn the dough out onto a lightly floured surface and gently knead it a few times until it forms a cohesive ball.
6. Pat the dough into a circle about 3/4-inch thick. Use a biscuit cutter or a glass to cut out biscuits, and place them on the prepared baking sheet.
7. Bake the biscuits for 12 to 15 minutes or until they are golden brown on top.

Ingredients for Filet Mignon and Red Wine Gravy:

- 2 filet mignon steaks, about 6-8 ounces each
- 2 tablespoons unsalted butter
- 1/4 cup finely chopped shallots
- 1 cup beef broth
- 1/2 cup red wine (such as Cabernet Sauvignon or Merlot)
- 1 tablespoon all-purpose flour
- Salt and freshly ground black pepper to taste
- Fresh thyme sprigs for garnish (optional)

Instructions for Filet Mignon and Red Wine Gravy:

1. Preheat your oven to 400°F (200°C).
2. Season the filet mignon steaks generously with salt and freshly ground black pepper.
3. In a large oven-safe skillet over medium-high heat, melt 1 tablespoon of unsalted butter. Add the filet mignon steaks to the skillet and sear them for about 2-3 minutes per side, or until they develop a golden crust.
4. Transfer the skillet to the preheated oven and roast the filet mignon steaks for about 5-7 minutes (for medium-rare), or until they reach your desired level of doneness.
5. Remove the skillet from the oven and transfer the filet mignon steaks to a plate. Cover them loosely with foil to keep them warm while you make the red wine gravy.
6. Place the skillet back on the stovetop over medium heat. Add the remaining 1 tablespoon of unsalted butter and sauté the finely chopped shallots until they become soft and translucent.
7. Stir in the all-purpose flour, and cook for a minute to eliminate the raw flour taste.
8. Gradually pour in the red wine and beef broth, stirring

constantly to prevent lumps from forming.

9. Let the gravy simmer until it thickens to your desired consistency. Season with salt and freshly ground black pepper to taste.

Assemble the Filet Mignon and Red Wine Gravy with Biscuits:

1. Split the freshly baked biscuits in half and place them on individual serving plates.
2. Place a cooked filet mignon steak on top of each biscuit.
3. Ladle a generous amount of the red wine gravy over the filet mignon.
4. Optionally, garnish with fresh thyme sprigs for added aroma and presentation.
5. Serve the Filet Mignon and Red Wine Gravy with Biscuits while warm, and savor the exquisite flavors of tender steak paired with a rich and flavorful red wine gravy.

10.3 Spinach and Artichoke Biscuits

These delectable biscuits are filled with the goodness of spinach and artichokes, creating a gourmet twist on the classic biscuit. With their delightful flavors and vibrant colors, these biscuits are a wonderful accompaniment to any meal or a standout side dish on their own.

Ingredients for Biscuits:

- 2 cups all-purpose flour
- 1 tablespoon baking powder
- 1/2 teaspoon baking soda
- 1 teaspoon salt
- 6 tablespoons cold unsalted butter, cut into small cubes
- 2/3 cup buttermilk
- 1/2 cup chopped cooked spinach (squeezed to remove excess moisture)
- 1/2 cup chopped artichoke hearts (canned or frozen, thawed and drained)

Instructions for Biscuits:

1. Preheat your oven to 450°F (230°C) and line a baking sheet with parchment paper.
2. In a large mixing bowl, whisk together the flour, baking powder, baking soda, and salt.
3. Add the cold butter cubes to the dry ingredients and use a pastry cutter or your fingertips to work the butter into the flour until the mixture resembles coarse crumbs.
4. Gradually pour in the buttermilk, stirring with a fork until the dough just comes together.
5. Gently fold in the chopped cooked spinach and chopped artichoke hearts until evenly distributed in the dough.
6. Turn the dough out onto a lightly floured surface and gently

knead it a few times until it forms a cohesive ball.

7. Pat the dough into a circle about 3/4-inch thick. Use a biscuit cutter or a glass to cut out biscuits, and place them on the prepared baking sheet.

8. Bake the biscuits for 12 to 15 minutes or until they are golden brown on top.

9. Serve the Spinach and Artichoke Biscuits warm, and enjoy their delightful flavors and vibrant colors that make them a gourmet treat for any meal.

In this chapter, we've explored gourmet biscuit meals that bring a touch of luxury and indulgence to your dining experience. From the elegant lobster bisque served over biscuits to the succulent filet mignon with red wine gravy, and the delectable spinach and artichoke biscuits, these gourmet creations showcase the versatility of biscuits in gourmet dishes that are perfect for special occasions or when you want to treat yourself to something extraordinary.

Chapter 11: Biscuit Desserts

In this chapter, we're diving into the sweet side of biscuits with delightful dessert creations. From the classic peach cobbler with biscuit topping to the indulgent chocolate-stuffed biscuits, and the refreshing berry shortcakes, these biscuit desserts are a treat for your taste buds and a perfect way to end any meal on a sweet note.

11.1 Peach Cobbler with Biscuit Topping

This classic Southern dessert brings together juicy, sweet peaches and a buttery biscuit topping that bakes to golden perfection. Served warm with a scoop of vanilla ice cream, it's a heartwarming and satisfying dessert that captures the essence of comfort.

Ingredients for Biscuit Topping:

- 1 cup all-purpose flour
- 2 tablespoons granulated sugar
- 1 1/2 teaspoons baking powder
- 1/4 teaspoon salt
- 1/4 cup cold unsalted butter, cut into small cubes
- 1/3 cup whole milk

Instructions for Biscuit Topping:

1. In a large mixing bowl, whisk together the flour, granulated sugar, baking powder, and salt.
2. Add the cold butter cubes to the dry ingredients and use a pastry cutter or your fingertips to work the butter into the flour until the mixture resembles coarse crumbs.
3. Gradually pour in the whole milk, stirring with a fork until the dough just comes together.

4. Turn the dough out onto a lightly floured surface and gently knead it a few times until it forms a cohesive ball.

5. Pat the dough into a circle about 1/2-inch thick. Use a biscuit cutter or a glass to cut out biscuits, and set them aside.

Ingredients for Peach Filling:

- 6 cups sliced and peeled fresh peaches (about 6-8 peaches)
- 1/2 cup granulated sugar
- 1 tablespoon cornstarch
- 1 teaspoon vanilla extract
- 1/4 teaspoon ground cinnamon
- 1/4 teaspoon ground nutmeg
- 1 tablespoon lemon juice

Instructions for Peach Filling:

1. Preheat your oven to 375°F (190°C). Grease a 9x13-inch baking dish.

2. In a large mixing bowl, combine the sliced peaches, granulated sugar, cornstarch, vanilla extract, ground cinnamon, ground nutmeg, and lemon juice. Toss the ingredients together until the peaches are coated evenly.

3. Transfer the peach mixture to the greased baking dish and spread it out evenly.

4. Arrange the biscuit dough on top of the peach filling, leaving a little space between each biscuit.

5. Bake the peach cobbler in the preheated oven for 25-30 minutes or until the biscuit topping is golden brown and the peach filling is bubbly.

6. Remove the peach cobbler from the oven and let it cool slightly before serving.

7. Serve the Peach Cobbler with Biscuit Topping warm, and

enjoy the luscious combination of sweet peaches and buttery biscuits.

11.2 Chocolate-Stuffed Biscuits

For a delectable and indulgent treat, these chocolate-stuffed biscuits are a delightful surprise. With a gooey chocolate center, they're perfect for satisfying your chocolate cravings and making any day feel like a special occasion.

Ingredients for Biscuits:

- 2 cups all-purpose flour
- 1 tablespoon baking powder
- 1/2 teaspoon baking soda
- 1 teaspoon salt
- 6 tablespoons cold unsalted butter, cut into small cubes
- 2/3 cup buttermilk
- 1/2 cup chocolate chips or chunks (semi-sweet or dark chocolate)

Instructions for Biscuits:

1. Preheat your oven to 450°F (230°C) and line a baking sheet with parchment paper.
2. In a large mixing bowl, whisk together the flour, baking powder, baking soda, and salt.
3. Add the cold butter cubes to the dry ingredients and use a pastry cutter or your fingertips to work the butter into the flour until the mixture resembles coarse crumbs.
4. Gradually pour in the buttermilk, stirring with a fork until the dough just comes together.
5. Gently fold in the chocolate chips or chunks until evenly distributed in the dough.

6. Turn the dough out onto a lightly floured surface and gently knead it a few times until it forms a cohesive ball.
7. Pat the dough into a circle about 3/4-inch thick. Use a biscuit cutter or a glass to cut out biscuits, and place them on the prepared baking sheet.
8. Bake the biscuits for 12 to 15 minutes or until they are golden brown on top.
9. Serve the Chocolate-Stuffed Biscuits warm, and savor the gooey chocolate surprise hidden inside each fluffy biscuit

11.3 Berry Shortcakes

These delightful berry shortcakes are a refreshing and fruity dessert that celebrates the season's best berries. With sweet and juicy berries sandwiched between tender biscuits and topped with whipped cream, it's a dessert that's both beautiful and delicious.

Ingredients for Biscuits:

- 2 cups all-purpose flour
- 1 tablespoon baking powder
- 1/2 teaspoon baking soda
- 1 teaspoon sugar
- 1/2 teaspoon salt
- 6 tablespoons cold unsalted butter, cut into small cubes
- 2/3 cup buttermilk

Instructions for Biscuits:

1. Preheat your oven to 450°F (230°C) and line a baking sheet with parchment paper.
2. In a large mixing bowl, whisk together the flour, baking powder, baking soda, sugar, and salt.
3. Add the cold butter cubes to the dry ingredients and use a

pastry cutter or your fingertips to work the butter into the flour until the mixture resembles coarse crumbs.

4. Gradually pour in the buttermilk, stirring with a fork until the dough just comes together.

5. Turn the dough out onto a lightly floured surface and gently knead it a few times until it forms a cohesive ball.

6. Pat the dough into a circle about 3/4-inch thick. Use a biscuit cutter or a glass to cut out biscuits, and place them on the prepared baking sheet.

7. Bake the biscuits for 12 to 15 minutes or until they are golden brown on top.

Ingredients for Berry Filling:

- 4 cups mixed fresh berries (strawberries, blueberries, raspberries, blackberries)
- 2 tablespoons granulated sugar
- 1 tablespoon lemon juice

Instructions for Berry Filling:

1. In a large mixing bowl, gently toss together the mixed fresh berries, granulated sugar, and lemon juice until the berries are coated with the sugar and lemon juice mixture.

2. Let the berry filling sit for about 15 minutes to allow the flavors to meld and the berries to release their juices.

3. Serve the Berry Shortcakes by splitting the freshly baked biscuits in half. Spoon the berry filling over the bottom half of each biscuit and top it with a dollop of whipped cream. Place the top half of the biscuit on the whipped cream, and optionally, garnish with a fresh berry on top for an extra touch of elegance.

Enjoy the Berry Shortcakes, and let the sweet and juicy berries combined with the tender biscuits and whipped cream take you on a delightful dessert journey.

In this chapter, we've explored sweet and delectable biscuit desserts that are perfect for satisfying your sweet tooth and ending any meal on a delightful note. From the classic peach cobbler with biscuit topping to the indulgent chocolate-stuffed biscuits, and the refreshing berry shortcakes, these biscuit desserts offer a variety of flavors and textures that will surely become favorites for dessert lovers.

Chapter 12: Hearty Gravy Combos

In this chapter, we're exploring hearty and comforting gravy combinations that take biscuits to the next level. From the classic country fried steak with creamy gravy to the innovative biscuit shepherd's pie, and the delicious turkey and stuffing biscuits, these savory dishes are perfect for satisfying your hunger and warming your soul.

12.1 Country Fried Steak with Creamy Gravy

This Southern classic pairs tenderized and breaded steak with a rich and creamy gravy, served over warm biscuits. It's a hearty and indulgent meal that brings together the best of comfort food in one delicious dish.

Ingredients for Biscuits:

- 2 cups all-purpose flour
- 1 tablespoon baking powder
- 1/2 teaspoon baking soda
- 1 teaspoon salt
- 6 tablespoons cold unsalted butter, cut into small cubes
- 2/3 cup buttermilk

Instructions for Biscuits:

1. Preheat your oven to 450°F (230°C) and line a baking sheet with parchment paper.
2. In a large mixing bowl, whisk together the flour, baking powder, baking soda, and salt.
3. Add the cold butter cubes to the dry ingredients and use a pastry cutter or your fingertips to work the butter into the

flour until the mixture resembles coarse crumbs.

4. Gradually pour in the buttermilk, stirring with a fork until the dough just comes together.
5. Turn the dough out onto a lightly floured surface and gently knead it a few times until it forms a cohesive ball.
6. Pat the dough into a circle about 3/4-inch thick. Use a biscuit cutter or a glass to cut out biscuits, and place them on the prepared baking sheet.
7. Bake the biscuits for 12 to 15 minutes or until they are golden brown on top.

Ingredients for Country Fried Steak and Creamy Gravy:

- 4 cube steaks (tenderized round steaks)
- 1 cup all-purpose flour
- 1 teaspoon salt
- 1/2 teaspoon black pepper
- 1/4 teaspoon garlic powder
- 1/4 teaspoon paprika
- 1/4 teaspoon cayenne pepper (optional, for added heat)
- 1 cup buttermilk
- Vegetable oil, for frying

Instructions for Country Fried Steak and Creamy Gravy:

1. In a shallow dish, combine the flour, salt, black pepper, garlic powder, paprika, and cayenne pepper (if using).
2. Dip each cube steak into the buttermilk, allowing any excess to drip off, and then dredge it in the seasoned flour mixture, pressing the flour onto the steak to adhere.
3. In a large skillet, heat enough vegetable oil to cover the bottom of the pan over medium heat.
4. Fry the breaded cube steaks for 3-4 minutes per side or until

they are golden brown and cooked through. Remove them from the skillet and place them on a plate lined with paper towels to drain any excess oil.

Ingredients for Creamy Gravy:

- 2 tablespoons unsalted butter
- 2 tablespoons all-purpose flour
- 2 cups whole milk
- Salt and freshly ground black pepper to taste

Instructions for Creamy Gravy:

1. In the same skillet used to fry the cube steaks, melt the unsalted butter over medium heat.
2. Sprinkle the all-purpose flour over the melted butter, stirring to create a roux. Cook for a minute or two to eliminate the raw flour taste.
3. Gradually pour in the whole milk, stirring constantly to prevent lumps from forming.
4. Cook the gravy until it thickens to your desired consistency. Season with salt and freshly ground black pepper to taste.

Assemble the Country Fried Steak with Creamy Gravy:

1. Split the freshly baked biscuits in half and place them on individual serving plates.
2. Top each biscuit half with a fried cube steak.
3. Drizzle a generous amount of the creamy gravy over the cube steak and biscuits.
4. Optionally, garnish with chopped fresh parsley for added freshness and presentation.

5. Serve the Country Fried Steak with Creamy Gravy while warm, and enjoy the hearty and comforting combination of tender steak and creamy gravy served over fluffy biscuits.

12.2 Biscuit Shepherd's Pie

This creative twist on the classic shepherd's pie replaces the traditional mashed potato topping with fluffy biscuits. The savory meat and vegetable filling, combined with the buttery biscuit topping, create a comforting and satisfying one-dish meal.

Ingredients for Biscuits:

- 2 cups all-purpose flour
- 1 tablespoon baking powder
- 1/2 teaspoon baking soda
- 1 teaspoon salt
- 6 tablespoons cold unsalted butter, cut into small cubes
- 2/3 cup buttermilk

Instructions for Biscuits:

1. Preheat your oven to 450°F (230°C) and line a baking sheet with parchment paper.
2. In a large mixing bowl, whisk together the flour, baking powder, baking soda, and salt.
3. Add the cold butter cubes to the dry ingredients and use a pastry cutter or your fingertips to work the butter into the flour until the mixture resembles coarse crumbs.
4. Gradually pour in the buttermilk, stirring with a fork until the dough just comes together.
5. Turn the dough out onto a lightly floured surface and gently knead it a few times until it forms a cohesive ball.
6. Pat the dough into a circle about 3/4-inch thick. Use a biscuit

cutter or a glass to cut out biscuits, and place them on the prepared baking sheet.

7. Bake the biscuits for 12 to 15 minutes or until they are golden brown on top.

Ingredients for Shepherd's Pie Filling:

- 1 pound ground beef or lamb
- 1 tablespoon vegetable oil
- 1 medium onion, diced
- 2 cloves garlic, minced
- 1 cup diced carrots
- 1 cup frozen peas
- 2 tablespoons tomato paste
- 1 cup beef or vegetable broth
- 2 teaspoons Worcestershire sauce
- Salt and freshly ground black pepper to taste

Instructions for Shepherd's Pie Filling:

1. In a large skillet over medium heat, heat the vegetable oil. Add the diced onion and minced garlic, and sauté until they become soft and fragrant.
2. Add the ground beef or lamb to the skillet and cook until it is browned and cooked through, breaking it apart with a spoon as it cooks.
3. Stir in the diced carrots and frozen peas, and cook for a few more minutes until the vegetables start to soften.
4. Add the tomato paste, beef or vegetable broth, and Worcestershire sauce to the skillet, stirring to combine all the ingredients.
5. Let the filling simmer for about 10-15 minutes or until the

liquid reduces and the mixture thickens. Season with salt and freshly ground black pepper to taste.

Assemble the Biscuit Shepherd's Pie:

1. Preheat your oven to 375°F (190°C).
2. Transfer the shepherd's pie filling to a greased 9x13-inch baking dish, spreading it out evenly.
3. Arrange the freshly baked biscuits on top of the filling, leaving a little space between each biscuit.
4. Bake the biscuit shepherd's pie in the preheated oven for 15-20 minutes or until the biscuits are heated through and lightly browned.
5. Serve the Biscuit Shepherd's Pie while warm, and enjoy the delicious and comforting combination of savory meat and vegetables topped with fluffy biscuits.

12.3 Turkey and Stuffing Biscuits

These delightful biscuits bring together the flavors of Thanksgiving in a handheld treat. Filled with tender turkey and savory stuffing, they're a perfect way to enjoy holiday flavors any time of the year.

Ingredients for Biscuits:

- 2 cups all-purpose flour
- 1 tablespoon baking powder
- 1/2 teaspoon baking soda
- 1 teaspoon salt
- 6 tablespoons cold unsalted butter, cut into small cubes
- 2/3 cup buttermilk

Instructions for Biscuits:

1. Preheat your oven to 450°F (230°C) and line a baking sheet with parchment paper.
2. In a large mixing bowl, whisk together the flour, baking powder, baking soda, and salt.
3. Add the cold butter cubes to the dry ingredients and use a pastry cutter or your fingertips to work the butter into the flour until the mixture resembles coarse crumbs.
4. Gradually pour in the buttermilk, stirring with a fork until the dough just comes together.
5. Turn the dough out onto a lightly floured surface and gently knead it a few times until it forms a cohesive ball.
6. Pat the dough into a circle about 3/4-inch thick. Use a biscuit cutter or a glass to cut out biscuits, and place them on the prepared baking sheet.
7. Bake the biscuits for 12 to 15 minutes or until they are golden brown on top.

Ingredients for Turkey and Stuffing Filling:

- 2 cups cooked and shredded turkey (leftover roast turkey works great)
- 1 1/2 cups prepared stuffing (leftover or store-bought)
- 1/2 cup turkey or chicken gravy (store-bought or homemade)
- Cranberry sauce for serving (optional)

Instructions for Turkey and Stuffing Filling:

1. In a medium mixing bowl, combine the shredded turkey, prepared stuffing, and turkey or chicken gravy. Mix until all the ingredients are well incorporated.

Assemble the Turkey and Stuffing Biscuits:

1. Preheat your oven to 350°F (175°C).
2. Split the freshly baked biscuits in half and place them on a baking sheet, cut side up.
3. Spoon a generous amount of the turkey and stuffing filling onto the bottom half of each biscuit.
4. Place the top half of each biscuit on the filling, pressing gently to secure the sandwich.
5. Optionally, warm the assembled biscuits in the preheated oven for a few minutes to ensure the filling is heated through.
6. Serve the Turkey and Stuffing Biscuits warm, and optionally, accompany them with a side of cranberry sauce for an extra burst of holiday flavor.

In this chapter, we've explored hearty and comforting gravy combinations that take biscuits to a new level of deliciousness. From the classic country fried steak with creamy gravy to the innovative biscuit shepherd's pie, and the delicious turkey and stuffing biscuits, these savory dishes offer a hearty and satisfying meal that's perfect for any time of the year.

Chapter 13: Quick and Easy Biscuits

In this chapter, we're exploring quick and easy biscuit recipes that are perfect for when you're short on time but still craving the comfort of freshly baked biscuits. From the convenient biscuit in a mug (microwave recipe) to the versatile biscuit flatbreads, and the delightful biscuit dumplings for stews, these recipes will save you time without sacrificing flavor.

13.1 Biscuit in a Mug (Microwave Recipe)

This single-serving biscuit in a mug recipe is a quick and convenient way to satisfy your biscuit cravings without using the oven. With just a few simple ingredients and a microwave, you can enjoy a warm and fluffy biscuit in minutes.

Ingredients:

- 4 tablespoons all-purpose flour
- 1/2 teaspoon baking powder
- 1/8 teaspoon salt
- 2 tablespoons milk
- 1 tablespoon vegetable oil or melted butter

Instructions:

1. In a microwave-safe mug, whisk together the all-purpose flour, baking powder, and salt.
2. Add the milk and vegetable oil or melted butter to the mug, stirring until the ingredients are well combined and form a smooth batter.
3. Microwave the mug on high for about 1 minute and 30

seconds to 2 minutes, or until the biscuit has risen and is cooked through.

4. Serve the Biscuit in a Mug while warm, and enjoy this quick and easy biscuit for a satisfying snack or a small breakfast treat.

13.2 Biscuit Flatbreads

These versatile biscuit flatbreads are a quick and easy alternative to traditional bread. With just a few ingredients, you can whip up these delightful flatbreads to accompany a variety of meals, from soups and salads to curries and stews.

Ingredients:

- 2 cups all-purpose flour
- 1 tablespoon baking powder
- 1/2 teaspoon salt
- 3/4 cup buttermilk
- 2 tablespoons vegetable oil or melted butter

Instructions:

1. In a large mixing bowl, whisk together the all-purpose flour, baking powder, and salt.
2. Gradually pour in the buttermilk, stirring with a fork until the dough comes together.
3. Turn the dough out onto a lightly floured surface and knead it gently a few times until it forms a smooth ball.
4. Divide the dough into 4 equal portions and roll each portion into a flat disc, about 1/4-inch thick.
5. Heat a skillet or griddle over medium-high heat and brush it with vegetable oil or melted butter.
6. Cook each flatbread for about 2-3 minutes on each side or until they are golden brown and cooked through.
7. Serve the Biscuit Flatbreads warm, and enjoy their versatility as a delicious accompaniment to various dishes.

13.3 Biscuit Dumplings for Stews

These quick and easy biscuit dumplings add a comforting touch to hearty stews and soups. With just a handful of ingredients, you can create fluffy and flavorful dumplings that turn any simple stew into a satisfying meal.

Ingredients:

- 1 cup all-purpose flour
- 2 teaspoons baking powder
- 1/2 teaspoon salt
- 1/2 cup milk
- 2 tablespoons melted butter

Instructions:

1. In a medium mixing bowl, whisk together the all-purpose flour, baking powder, and salt.

2. Gradually pour in the milk and melted butter, stirring until the ingredients form a sticky dough.
3. Drop spoonfuls of the biscuit dumpling dough directly into a simmering stew or soup, spacing them out evenly.
4. Cover the pot and let the dumplings cook for about 15-20 minutes, or until they are cooked through and have expanded in size.
5. Serve the Biscuit Dumplings for Stews while warm, and enjoy the comforting addition they bring to your favorite hearty soups and stews.

In this chapter, we've explored quick and easy biscuit recipes that are perfect for those times when you want a delicious biscuit without the fuss. From the convenient biscuit in a mug (microwave recipe) to the versatile biscuit flatbreads, and the delightful biscuit dumplings for stews, these recipes offer a range of flavors and textures that are sure to become favorites for quick and satisfying meals.

Chapter 14: Sausage Variations

In this chapter, we're exploring a variety of sausage-based gravy combinations that take biscuits to new levels of flavor. From the bold and spicy chorizo gravy to the sweet and savory maple breakfast sausage biscuits, and the delightful Italian sausage and peppers gravy, these sausage variations offer a delicious twist to the classic biscuit and gravy combination.

14.1 Spicy Chorizo Gravy

This bold and flavorful chorizo gravy is a delicious twist on traditional sausage gravy. With its rich and spicy profile, it adds a kick of heat and a burst of exciting flavors to your biscuits.

Ingredients for Chorizo Gravy:

- 8 ounces chorizo sausage, removed from casings
- 2 tablespoons unsalted butter
- 1/4 cup all-purpose flour
- 2 cups whole milk
- 1/4 teaspoon cayenne pepper (adjust to your desired level of spiciness)
- Salt and freshly ground black pepper to taste
- Chopped fresh cilantro or green onions for garnish (optional)

Instructions for Chorizo Gravy:

1. In a large skillet over medium heat, cook the chorizo sausage, breaking it apart with a spoon, until it is browned and cooked through.
2. Remove the cooked chorizo from the skillet and set it aside on a plate lined with paper towels to drain any excess oil.

3. In the same skillet, melt the unsalted butter over medium heat.

4. Stir in the all-purpose flour, and cook for a minute or two to eliminate the raw flour taste.

5. Gradually pour in the whole milk, stirring constantly to prevent lumps from forming.

6. Add the cooked chorizo back into the skillet, and season with cayenne pepper, salt, and freshly ground black pepper to taste.

7. Let the gravy simmer until it thickens to your desired consistency.

8. Serve the Spicy Chorizo Gravy over freshly baked biscuits, and optionally, garnish with chopped fresh cilantro or green onions for added freshness and presentation.

14.2 Maple Breakfast Sausage Biscuits

This sweet and savory combination of maple-flavored breakfast sausage and tender biscuits is a delightful treat for breakfast or brunch. The harmonious blend of flavors will surely become a favorite morning indulgence.

Ingredients for Maple Breakfast Sausage Biscuits:

- 1 pound ground breakfast sausage (pork or turkey)
- 2 tablespoons maple syrup
- 2 cups all-purpose flour
- 1 tablespoon baking powder
- 1/2 teaspoon baking soda
- 1 teaspoon salt
- 6 tablespoons cold unsalted butter, cut into small cubes
- 2/3 cup buttermilk

Instructions for Maple Breakfast Sausage Biscuits:

1. Preheat your oven to 450°F (230°C) and line a baking sheet

with parchment paper.

2. In a medium mixing bowl, combine the ground breakfast sausage and maple syrup, mixing until the maple syrup is evenly distributed throughout the sausage.

3. In a separate large mixing bowl, whisk together the all-purpose flour, baking powder, baking soda, and salt.

4. Add the cold butter cubes to the dry ingredients and use a pastry cutter or your fingertips to work the butter into the flour until the mixture resembles coarse crumbs.

5. Gradually pour in the buttermilk, stirring with a fork until the dough just comes together.

6. Turn the dough out onto a lightly floured surface and gently knead it a few times until it forms a cohesive ball.

7. Pat the dough into a circle about 3/4-inch thick. Use a biscuit cutter or a glass to cut out biscuits, and place them on the prepared baking sheet.

8. Place a spoonful of the maple breakfast sausage mixture on top of each biscuit, pressing it gently into the dough.

9. Bake the biscuits for 12 to 15 minutes or until they are golden brown and the sausage is cooked through.

10. Serve the Maple Breakfast Sausage Biscuits warm, and enjoy the sweet and savory combination that's perfect for a delicious breakfast or brunch.

14.3 Italian Sausage and Peppers Gravy

This hearty and flavorful Italian sausage and peppers gravy is a delightful twist on traditional sausage gravy. With the addition of sautéed peppers and onions, it brings the taste of Italy to your biscuits.

Ingredients for Italian Sausage and Peppers Gravy:

- 1 pound Italian sausage (sweet or hot), removed from casings

- 1 tablespoon olive oil
- 1 bell pepper (any color), thinly sliced
- 1 small onion, thinly sliced
- 2 tablespoons all-purpose flour
- 2 cups beef or chicken broth
- 1/2 cup heavy cream
- Salt and freshly ground black pepper to taste
- Fresh basil leaves for garnish (optional)

Instructions for Italian Sausage and Peppers Gravy:

1. In a large skillet over medium heat, cook the Italian sausage, breaking it apart with a spoon, until it is browned and cooked through.
2. Remove the cooked sausage from the skillet and set it aside on a plate lined with paper towels to drain any excess oil.
3. In the same skillet, heat the olive oil over medium heat. Add the thinly sliced bell pepper and onion, and sauté until they become soft and slightly caramelized.
4. Stir in the all-purpose flour, and cook for a minute or two to eliminate the raw flour taste.
5. Gradually pour in the beef or chicken broth, stirring constantly to prevent lumps from forming.
6. Add the cooked sausage back into the skillet, and let the gravy simmer for a few minutes to allow the flavors to meld.
7. Stir in the heavy cream and season with salt and freshly ground black pepper to taste.
8. Serve the Italian Sausage and Peppers Gravy over freshly baked biscuits, and optionally, garnish with fresh basil leaves for added aroma and presentation.

In this chapter, we've explored a variety of sausage-based gravy combinations that elevate the classic biscuit and gravy pairing to new heights of flavor. From the bold and spicy chorizo gravy to the sweet and savory maple breakfast sausage biscuits, and the delightful Italian sausage and peppers gravy, these sausage variations offer a range of exciting tastes that will delight your taste buds.

Chapter 15: Biscuits for Special Diets

In this chapter, we're exploring biscuit recipes tailored to special diets, offering delicious alternatives for those following specific dietary restrictions. From the keto-friendly almond flour biscuits to the paleo sweet potato biscuits, and the gluten-free biscuits and mushroom gravy, these recipes ensure that everyone can enjoy the comforting taste of biscuits and gravy, regardless of dietary requirements.

15.1 Keto-Friendly Almond Flour Biscuits

These keto-friendly biscuits use almond flour instead of traditional all-purpose flour, making them low in carbs and suitable for those following a ketogenic diet. Enjoy these tender and nutty biscuits guilt-free, knowing they align with your dietary goals.

Ingredients for Keto-Friendly Almond Flour Biscuits:

- 2 cups almond flour
- 1 tablespoon baking powder
- 1/2 teaspoon salt
- 4 tablespoons cold unsalted butter, cut into small cubes
- 2 large eggs
- 1/4 cup sour cream or Greek yogurt

Instructions for Keto-Friendly Almond Flour Biscuits:

1. Preheat your oven to 350°F (175°C) and line a baking sheet with parchment paper.
2. In a large mixing bowl, whisk together the almond flour, baking powder, and salt.
3. Add the cold butter cubes to the dry ingredients and use a pastry cutter or your fingertips to work the butter into the

almond flour until the mixture resembles coarse crumbs.

4. In a separate small bowl, whisk together the eggs and sour cream or Greek yogurt.

5. Gradually pour the egg mixture into the almond flour mixture, stirring until a thick dough forms.

6. Turn the dough out onto a piece of parchment paper and gently shape it into a circle about 1/2-inch thick.

7. Use a biscuit cutter or a glass to cut out biscuits, and place them on the prepared baking sheet.

8. Bake the biscuits for 15 to 18 minutes or until they are golden brown and cooked through.

9. Serve the Keto-Friendly Almond Flour Biscuits warm, and savor their nutty flavor and tender texture, knowing they fit perfectly into your ketogenic lifestyle.

15.2 Paleo Sweet Potato Biscuits

For those following a paleo diet, these sweet potato biscuits are a delightful alternative. Made with sweet potatoes and paleo-friendly ingredients, these biscuits are both nutritious and delicious.

Ingredients for Paleo Sweet Potato Biscuits:

- 1 cup cooked and mashed sweet potato (about 1 medium sweet potato)
- 1/4 cup coconut flour
- 1/4 cup almond flour
- 1/4 cup arrowroot flour or tapioca flour
- 1 teaspoon baking powder
- 1/2 teaspoon baking soda
- 1/4 teaspoon salt
- 2 large eggs
- 2 tablespoons melted coconut oil
- 1 tablespoon honey (optional, for a touch of sweetness)

Instructions for Paleo Sweet Potato Biscuits:

1. Preheat your oven to 350°F (175°C) and line a baking sheet with parchment paper.
2. In a large mixing bowl, whisk together the coconut flour, almond flour, arrowroot flour or tapioca flour, baking powder, baking soda, and salt.
3. In a separate bowl, combine the mashed sweet potato, eggs, melted coconut oil, and honey (if using).
4. Gradually pour the wet ingredients into the dry ingredients, stirring until a thick and sticky dough forms.
5. Turn the dough out onto a piece of parchment paper and gently shape it into a circle about 1/2-inch thick.
6. Use a biscuit cutter or a glass to cut out biscuits, and place them on the prepared baking sheet.

7. Bake the biscuits for 15 to 18 minutes or until they are lightly golden and cooked through.
8. Serve the Paleo Sweet Potato Biscuits warm, and enjoy their natural sweetness and soft texture, perfect for anyone following a paleo lifestyle.

15.3 Gluten-Free Biscuits and Mushroom Gravy

For those with gluten sensitivities or celiac disease, these gluten-free biscuits paired with a flavorful mushroom gravy offer a comforting and satisfying meal that's safe to enjoy.

Ingredients for Gluten-Free Biscuits:

- 1 1/2 cups gluten-free all-purpose flour blend (with xanthan gum, if not already included)
- 1 tablespoon baking powder
- 1/2 teaspoon salt
- 4 tablespoons cold unsalted butter, cut into small cubes
- 2/3 cup buttermilk

Instructions for Gluten-Free Biscuits:

1. Preheat your oven to 450°F (230°C) and line a baking sheet with parchment paper.
2. In a large mixing bowl, whisk together the gluten-free all-purpose flour blend, baking powder, and salt.
3. Add the cold butter cubes to the dry ingredients and use a pastry cutter or your fingertips to work the butter into the flour until the mixture resembles coarse crumbs.
4. Gradually pour in the buttermilk, stirring with a fork until the dough just comes together.
5. Turn the dough out onto a lightly floured surface. If the dough is too sticky, you can lightly dust it with additional gluten-free flour.

6. Gently knead the dough a few times until it forms a cohesive ball.
7. Pat the dough into a circle about 3/4-inch thick. Use a biscuit cutter or a glass to cut out biscuits, and place them on the prepared baking sheet.
8. Bake the biscuits for 12 to 15 minutes or until they are golden brown on top.

Ingredients for Mushroom Gravy:

- 8 ounces mushrooms (button or cremini), sliced
- 2 tablespoons unsalted butter
- 2 tablespoons gluten-free all-purpose flour blend (with xanthan gum, if not already included)
- 2 cups beef or vegetable broth
- 1/4 cup heavy cream
- Salt and freshly ground black pepper to taste
- Chopped fresh parsley for garnish (optional)

Instructions for Mushroom Gravy:

1. In a large skillet over medium heat, melt the unsalted butter.
2. Add the sliced mushrooms to the skillet and sauté until they are tender and lightly browned.
3. Stir in the gluten-free all-purpose flour blend, and cook for a minute or two to eliminate the raw flour taste.
4. Gradually pour in the beef or vegetable broth, stirring constantly to prevent lumps from forming.
5. Let the gravy simmer until it thickens to your desired consistency.
6. Stir in the heavy cream and season with salt and freshly ground black pepper to taste.
7. Serve the Gluten-Free Biscuits warm, and top them

generously with the flavorful Mushroom Gravy. Optionally, garnish with chopped fresh parsley for added freshness and presentation.

In this chapter, we've explored biscuit recipes tailored to special diets, providing delicious options for those following keto, paleo, or gluten-free lifestyles. From the keto-friendly almond flour biscuits to the paleo sweet potato biscuits, and the gluten-free biscuits and mushroom gravy, these recipes cater to various dietary requirements without compromising on taste and comfort.

Chapter 16: Gravy for Every Occasion

In this chapter, we're exploring a variety of gravy recipes that are perfect for different occasions, adding a touch of flavor and elegance to your meals. From the traditional holiday turkey gravy to the hearty game day chili gravy, and the sophisticated wine and shallot gravy, these recipes will elevate your dining experience for every special occasion.

16.1 Holiday Turkey Gravy

This classic holiday turkey gravy is the perfect accompaniment to your Thanksgiving or Christmas feast. Made with rich turkey drippings and savory flavors, it brings out the best in your roasted turkey and complements your holiday meal.

Ingredients for Holiday Turkey Gravy:

- 1/4 cup unsalted butter
- 1/4 cup all-purpose flour
- 2 cups turkey or chicken broth
- 1 cup turkey drippings (from roasted turkey)
- Salt and freshly ground black pepper to taste

Instructions for Holiday Turkey Gravy:

1. After roasting your turkey, transfer it to a carving board to rest. Place the roasting pan on the stovetop over medium heat.
2. Melt the unsalted butter in the roasting pan, scraping up any browned bits from the bottom of the pan.
3. Sprinkle the all-purpose flour over the melted butter, stirring to create a roux. Cook for a minute or two to eliminate the raw flour taste.

4. Gradually pour in the turkey or chicken broth and turkey drippings, stirring constantly to combine all the ingredients.

5. Let the gravy simmer until it thickens to your desired consistency. Season with salt and freshly ground black pepper to taste.

6. Serve the Holiday Turkey Gravy warm, and drizzle it over slices of roasted turkey and fluffy biscuits for a memorable holiday feast.

16.2 Game Day Chili Gravy

This hearty chili gravy is the perfect addition to your game day spread. Made with flavorful chili meat and spices, it adds a zesty kick to your biscuits, making them a crowd-pleasing favorite on game day.

Ingredients for Game Day Chili Gravy:

- 1 pound ground beef or turkey
- 1 small onion, finely chopped
- 2 cloves garlic, minced
- 1 tablespoon chili powder
- 1 teaspoon ground cumin
- 1/2 teaspoon paprika
- 1/4 teaspoon cayenne pepper (adjust to your desired level of spiciness)
- 1 cup beef broth
- 1/4 cup tomato sauce or crushed tomatoes
- Salt and freshly ground black pepper to taste

Instructions for Game Day Chili Gravy:

1. In a large skillet over medium heat, cook the ground beef or turkey until it is browned and cooked through.

2. Add the chopped onion and minced garlic to the skillet, and sauté until they become soft and fragrant.

3. Stir in the chili powder, ground cumin, paprika, and cayenne pepper, coating the meat and vegetables with the spices.

4. Pour in the beef broth and tomato sauce or crushed tomatoes, stirring to combine all the ingredients.

5. Let the gravy simmer for about 10 minutes or until it thickens and the flavors meld. Season with salt and freshly ground black pepper to taste.

6. Serve the Game Day Chili Gravy over warm biscuits, and enjoy the bold and zesty flavor that's perfect for cheering on your favorite team.

16.3 Elegant Wine and Shallot Gravy

This sophisticated wine and shallot gravy is a luxurious addition to your elegant dinner parties or special occasions. With the subtle sweetness of shallots and the rich depth of red wine, this gravy adds an indulgent touch to your biscuits.

Ingredients for Wine and Shallot Gravy:

- 2 tablespoons unsalted butter
- 1/4 cup finely chopped shallots
- 1 cup red wine (such as merlot or cabernet sauvignon)
- 1 cup beef or chicken broth
- 1/2 cup heavy cream
- Salt and freshly ground black pepper to taste
- Fresh thyme leaves for garnish (optional)

Instructions for Wine and Shallot Gravy:

1. In a saucepan over medium heat, melt the unsalted butter.

2. Add the finely chopped shallots to the saucepan, and sauté until they become soft and lightly caramelized.

3. Pour in the red wine, stirring to deglaze the pan and incorporate the flavors of the shallots.

4. Let the wine simmer and reduce by about half, intensifying the flavors.
5. Gradually pour in the beef or chicken broth and heavy cream, stirring constantly to combine all the ingredients.
6. Let the gravy simmer until it thickens to your desired consistency. Season with salt and freshly ground black pepper to taste.
7. Serve the Wine and Shallot Gravy over warm biscuits, and optionally, garnish with fresh thyme leaves for an elegant presentation that's perfect for your special occasions.

In this chapter, we've explored a variety of gravy recipes that cater to different occasions, adding a touch of flavor and elegance to your meals. From the traditional holiday turkey gravy to the hearty game day chili gravy, and the sophisticated wine and shallot gravy, these recipes ensure that you can enjoy the perfect gravy to complement your biscuits for every special moment.

Chapter 17: Biscuit Brunch Ideas

In this chapter, we're exploring creative and delicious biscuit brunch ideas that will make your weekend mornings extra special. From setting up a biscuit and gravy bar to indulging in biscuit French toast and enjoying flavorful biscuit breakfast tacos, these recipes will elevate your brunch experience and impress your guests.

17.1 Biscuit and Gravy Bar

Create an interactive and delightful brunch experience with a biscuit and gravy bar. Set up a buffet-style spread with a variety of biscuits and gravy options, along with an array of toppings and accompaniments, allowing everyone to customize their ultimate biscuit and gravy combination.

Biscuit Options:

- Classic buttermilk biscuits
- Flavored variations (e.g., cheddar, herbs)
- Keto-friendly almond flour biscuits
- Gluten-free biscuits

Gravy Options:

- Traditional sausage gravy
- Spicy chorizo gravy
- Mushroom and onion gravy

Toppings and Accompaniments:

- Scrambled eggs
- Crumbled bacon or sausage
- Sauteed vegetables (bell peppers, onions, spinach, etc.)

- Shredded cheese (cheddar, mozzarella, etc.)
- Fresh herbs (parsley, chives, etc.)
- Hot sauce or chili flakes for extra heat
- Invite your guests to assemble their own biscuit and gravy creations, making it a fun and flavorful experience for everyone.

17.2 Biscuit French Toast

Transform leftover biscuits into a delightful sweet brunch treat with this biscuit French toast recipe. The slightly crisp exterior and tender interior make these French toast biscuits a delectable and unique addition to your brunch table.

Ingredients for Biscuit French Toast:

- Leftover biscuits (at least a day old)
- 3 large eggs
- 1/2 cup milk
- 1 teaspoon vanilla extract
- Pinch of salt
- Butter or oil for cooking

Instructions for Biscuit French Toast:

1. In a shallow bowl or baking dish, whisk together the eggs, milk, vanilla extract, and a pinch of salt.
2. Dip each biscuit into the egg mixture, ensuring both sides are coated.
3. Heat a skillet or griddle over medium heat and add a pat of butter or a drizzle of oil.
4. Cook the dipped biscuits on the skillet or griddle for a few minutes on each side until they are golden brown and cooked through.
5. Serve the Biscuit French Toast warm, and drizzle with maple

syrup, honey, or a sprinkle of powdered sugar for a delightful sweet brunch treat.

17.3 Biscuit Breakfast Tacos

Combine the best of both worlds with these savory and satisfying biscuit breakfast tacos. Fill your biscuits with flavorful breakfast ingredients for a portable and delicious brunch option.

Ingredients for Biscuit Breakfast Tacos:

- Biscuits (homemade or store-bought)
- Scrambled eggs
- Cooked breakfast sausage or bacon
- Shredded cheese
- Sliced avocado
- Fresh salsa or pico de gallo
- Chopped cilantro

Instructions for Biscuit Breakfast Tacos:

1. Split the biscuits in half to create taco shells.
2. Fill each biscuit with a generous amount of scrambled eggs and your choice of cooked breakfast sausage or bacon.
3. Top with shredded cheese, sliced avocado, fresh salsa or pico de gallo, and chopped cilantro.
4. Serve the Biscuit Breakfast Tacos warm, and enjoy the combination of savory and fresh flavors for a satisfying and portable brunch option.

In this chapter, we've explored creative biscuit brunch ideas that are sure to impress your guests and make your brunches extra special. From setting up a biscuit and gravy bar to transforming leftover biscuits into delightful biscuit French toast and creating flavorful biscuit breakfast tacos, these recipes offer a range of options to elevate your weekend brunches.

Chapter 18: Vegetarian and Vegan Biscuit Feasts

In this chapter, we're celebrating the delicious flavors of vegetarian and vegan cuisine with biscuit feasts that cater to plant-based diets. From the hearty vegan sausage and mushroom gravy to the savory spinach and feta stuffed biscuits, and the nutritious lentil and vegetable biscuits, these recipes offer a range of options that are both satisfying and compassionate.

18.1 Vegan Sausage and Mushroom Gravy

This flavorful vegan sausage and mushroom gravy is a plant-based twist on traditional sausage gravy. Made with vegan sausage and sautéed mushrooms, it offers a rich and hearty topping for your biscuits.

Ingredients for Vegan Sausage and Mushroom Gravy:

- 8 ounces vegan sausage (store-bought or homemade)
- 1 tablespoon olive oil
- 8 ounces mushrooms, sliced
- 2 tablespoons all-purpose flour
- 2 cups vegetable broth
- 1 cup unsweetened plant-based milk (such as almond or soy milk)
- 1 teaspoon soy sauce or tamari
- Salt and freshly ground black pepper to taste
- Chopped fresh parsley for garnish (optional)

Instructions for Vegan Sausage and Mushroom Gravy:

1. In a skillet over medium heat, crumble the vegan sausage and

cook it until it is browned and cooked through.

2. Remove the cooked vegan sausage from the skillet and set it aside.

3. In the same skillet, heat the olive oil over medium heat. Add the sliced mushrooms and sauté until they become tender and lightly browned.

4. Stir in the all-purpose flour, and cook for a minute or two to eliminate the raw flour taste.

5. Gradually pour in the vegetable broth and plant-based milk, stirring constantly to combine all the ingredients.

6. Add the cooked vegan sausage back into the skillet and stir in the soy sauce or tamari.

7. Let the gravy simmer until it thickens to your desired consistency. Season with salt and freshly ground black pepper to taste.

8. Serve the Vegan Sausage and Mushroom Gravy over warm biscuits, and optionally, garnish with chopped fresh parsley for added freshness and presentation.

18.2 Spinach and Feta Stuffed Biscuits

These savory spinach and feta stuffed biscuits are a delightful combination of flavors and textures. With a flavorful spinach and feta filling inside tender biscuits, they make a delicious addition to your vegetarian biscuit feast.

Ingredients for Spinach and Feta Stuffed Biscuits:

- 2 cups all-purpose flour
- 1 tablespoon baking powder
- 1/2 teaspoon baking soda
- 1 teaspoon salt
- 4 tablespoons cold unsalted butter, cut into small cubes
- 1 cup buttermilk
- 1 cup cooked and drained chopped spinach (squeezed to

remove excess water)
- 1/2 cup crumbled feta cheese
- 1/4 cup chopped green onions

Instructions for Spinach and Feta Stuffed Biscuits:

1. Preheat your oven to 450°F (230°C) and line a baking sheet with parchment paper.
2. In a large mixing bowl, whisk together the all-purpose flour, baking powder, baking soda, and salt.
3. Add the cold butter cubes to the dry ingredients and use a pastry cutter or your fingertips to work the butter into the flour until the mixture resembles coarse crumbs.
4. Gradually pour in the buttermilk, stirring with a fork until the dough just comes together.
5. In a separate bowl, combine the cooked and drained chopped spinach, crumbled feta cheese, and chopped green onions.
6. On a lightly floured surface, roll out the biscuit dough to about 1/2-inch thickness. Cut the dough into circles using a biscuit cutter or a glass.
7. Place a spoonful of the spinach and feta filling in the center of each biscuit circle. Fold the edges of the biscuit dough over the filling and pinch them together to seal the biscuits.
8. Place the stuffed biscuits on the prepared baking sheet and bake for 12 to 15 minutes or until they are golden brown and cooked through.
9. Serve the Spinach and Feta Stuffed Biscuits warm, and savor the delightful combination of savory flavors in every bite.

18.3 Lentil and Vegetable Biscuits

These nutritious lentil and vegetable biscuits are packed with plant-based goodness. Filled with cooked lentils and a medley of vegetables, they are a hearty and wholesome addition to your vegetarian biscuit feast.

Ingredients for Lentil and Vegetable Biscuits:

- 1 cup cooked and drained lentils
- 1 tablespoon olive oil
- 1 small onion, finely chopped
- 1 carrot, grated
- 1/2 cup finely chopped bell peppers (any color)
- 1 teaspoon dried thyme
- 1 teaspoon dried oregano
- Salt and freshly ground black pepper to taste
- 2 cups all-purpose flour
- 1 tablespoon baking powder
- 1/2 teaspoon baking soda
- 1 teaspoon salt
- 4 tablespoons cold unsalted butter, cut into small cubes
- 1 cup buttermilk

Instructions for Lentil and Vegetable Biscuits:

1. Preheat your oven to 450°F (230°C) and line a baking sheet with parchment paper.
2. In a skillet over medium heat, heat the olive oil. Add the chopped onion, grated carrot, and finely chopped bell peppers. Sauté until the vegetables become soft and lightly caramelized.
3. Stir in the cooked and drained lentils, dried thyme, dried oregano, salt, and freshly ground black pepper. Cook for a few minutes to allow the flavors to meld. Remove from heat and let the lentil and vegetable mixture cool slightly.
4. In a large mixing bowl, whisk together the all-purpose flour, baking powder, baking soda, and salt.

5. Add the cold butter cubes to the dry ingredients and use a pastry cutter or your fingertips to work the butter into the flour until the mixture resembles coarse crumbs.
6. Gradually pour in the buttermilk, stirring with a fork until the dough just comes together.
7. On a lightly floured surface, roll out the biscuit dough to about 1/2-inch thickness. Cut the dough into circles using a biscuit cutter or a glass.
8. Place a spoonful of the lentil and vegetable mixture in the center of each biscuit circle. Fold the edges of the biscuit dough over the filling and pinch them together to seal the biscuits.
9. Place the stuffed biscuits on the prepared baking sheet and bake for 12 to 15 minutes or until they are golden brown and cooked through.
10. Serve the Lentil and Vegetable Biscuits warm, and enjoy the nourishing combination of lentils and vegetables in every bite.

In this chapter, we've celebrated the flavors of vegetarian and vegan cuisine with biscuit feasts that are both satisfying and compassionate. From the hearty vegan sausage and mushroom gravy to the savory spinach and feta stuffed biscuits, and the nutritious lentil and vegetable biscuits, these recipes offer a range of options to delight your taste buds and nourish your body.

Chapter 19: Biscuit Baking Troubleshooting

In this chapter, we'll address common biscuit baking mistakes and offer helpful fixes to ensure your biscuits turn out perfectly every time. Additionally, we'll provide tips for achieving the ideal consistency for your gravy, so you can enjoy a flawless biscuits and gravy experience.

19.1 Common Biscuit Baking Mistakes and Fixes

Mistake 1: Dense and Heavy Biscuits

Possible Causes: Overmixing the dough or using too much flour can result in tough and heavy biscuits.

Fix: Handle the dough as little as possible, and be sure not to overmix it. Use a gentle folding motion when incorporating the wet and dry ingredients. Also, measure the flour accurately, using a light hand when scooping the flour into the measuring cup and leveling it off.

Mistake 2: Biscuits Don't Rise Properly

Possible Causes: Using expired or old baking powder, or not using enough baking powder, can lead to biscuits that don't rise well.

Fix: Check the expiration date of your baking powder and ensure it's fresh. Also, make sure to use the right amount of baking powder according to the recipe. Baking powder is the leavening agent responsible for the rise in biscuits, so it's essential to use it correctly.

Mistake 3: Flat and Spreading Biscuits

Possible Causes: Soft or warm butter, or rolling the dough too thin, can cause biscuits to spread and lose their height during baking.

Fix: Make sure the butter is cold and firm when incorporating it into the dough. If necessary, chill the dough for a few minutes before cutting out the biscuits. Additionally, roll the dough to the specified thickness in the recipe to maintain the desired height.

Mistake 4: Biscuits Have a Tough Exterior

Possible Causes: Baking the biscuits at too high a temperature can cause the exterior to become tough before the interior is fully cooked.

Fix: Bake the biscuits at the recommended temperature in the recipe. Generally, baking biscuits at a high temperature, such as 450°F (230°C), ensures a golden exterior and a tender interior.

19.2 Perfecting Your Gravy Consistency

Creating the ideal gravy consistency can be a bit tricky, but with the right techniques, you can achieve a smooth and luscious gravy every time.

Tips for Perfecting Gravy Consistency:

Roux: The roux, a mixture of fat (butter or oil) and flour, is essential for thickening the gravy. When making the roux, cook it for a minute or two to eliminate the raw flour taste before adding the liquid.

Gradual Liquid Addition: When adding liquid (broth, milk, etc.) to the roux, do it gradually while stirring continuously. This helps prevent lumps from forming in the gravy.

Simmer and Thicken: Let the gravy simmer gently until it reaches your desired thickness. Keep in mind that the gravy will continue to thicken slightly as it cools.

Adjust Consistency: If your gravy becomes too thick, you can add more liquid (broth, milk, etc.) to thin it out. On the other hand, if it's too thin, you can continue simmering until it reduces and thickens further.

Cornstarch Slurry: If you prefer a gluten-free option for thickening your gravy, you can use a cornstarch slurry. Mix cornstarch with a small amount of cold liquid (water or broth) until smooth, and then gradually stir it into the hot gravy. Continue simmering until it thickens.

Adjust Seasoning: As the gravy thickens, taste and adjust the seasoning (salt, pepper, herbs, etc.) to your preference.

By following these tips, you'll be able to achieve the perfect gravy consistency to complement your delicious biscuits.

In this chapter, we've addressed common biscuit baking mistakes and offered fixes to ensure your biscuits turn out perfect every time. We've also provided tips for achieving the ideal consistency for your gravy, so you can enjoy a smooth and flavorful biscuits and gravy experience.

Chapter 20: Biscuits and Gravy Beyond Breakfast

In this chapter, we'll explore creative ways to enjoy biscuits and gravy for lunch and dinner, including leftover makeovers and freezing and reheating tips to make the most of this comforting dish throughout the week.

20.1 Creative Lunch and Dinner Ideas

Biscuits and gravy can be a versatile and satisfying dish for lunch and dinner. Here are some creative ideas to enjoy this classic comfort food beyond breakfast:

Biscuit Pot Pie: Use leftover biscuits as a savory crust for a delicious pot pie. Fill a casserole dish with your favorite pot pie filling, such as chicken and vegetables, or a vegetarian option with mushrooms and spinach. Top the filling with halved biscuits and bake until the biscuits are golden brown and the filling is bubbly.

Biscuit Sliders: Turn biscuits into mini sliders for a fun and flavorful lunch or dinner. Fill the biscuits with your choice of protein, such as pulled pork, barbecue jackfruit, or crispy tofu, along with coleslaw or pickles for added crunch and tang.

Biscuit Pizzas: Transform biscuits into mini pizzas by topping them with tomato sauce, cheese, and your favorite pizza toppings. Bake until the cheese is melted and bubbly, and the biscuits are crispy.

Biscuit Sandwiches: Create hearty sandwiches by splitting biscuits in half and filling them with your favorite deli meats, cheeses, and fresh veggies. Add some condiments like mayo, mustard, or pesto for extra flavor.

Biscuit Empanadas: Use biscuit dough to make empanadas filled with savory fillings like seasoned ground beef, black beans, and diced peppers. Seal the edges and bake until golden brown and delicious.

20.2 Leftover Makeovers

Leftover biscuits and gravy can be repurposed into new and exciting dishes. Here are some creative leftover makeovers:

Biscuit Croutons: Dice leftover biscuits into small cubes and toast them in the oven until they become crispy. Use these biscuit croutons to add a unique twist to your salads or soups.

Biscuit Stuffing: Crumble leftover biscuits and use them as a base for a flavorful stuffing. Mix in sautéed vegetables, herbs, and broth before baking until golden and aromatic.

Biscuit Dumplings: Tear or cut leftover biscuits into pieces and add them to a simmering stew or soup to create delicious biscuit dumplings. Let them cook until they puff up and become tender.

Biscuit Breakfast Hash: Crumble leftover biscuits and use them as a base for a hearty breakfast hash. Sauté diced potatoes, onions, and bell peppers in a skillet, then add the crumbled biscuits and your choice of protein like breakfast sausage or tofu.

20.3 Freezing and Reheating Tips

If you have leftover biscuits and gravy or want to prepare them in advance, here are some freezing and reheating tips:

Freezing Biscuits: Allow the biscuits to cool completely, then place them in an airtight container or a resealable freezer bag. Label the container with the date, and they can be stored in the freezer for up to three months.

Reheating Biscuits: To reheat frozen biscuits, preheat your oven to 350°F (175°C). Place the biscuits on a baking sheet and bake for 10 to 15 minutes or until they are warmed through and crispy on the outside.

Freezing Gravy: Allow the gravy to cool completely, then transfer it to an airtight container or a freezer-safe bag. Label the container with the date, and it can be stored in the freezer for up to three months.

Reheating Gravy: Thaw the frozen gravy in the refrigerator overnight. Reheat it gently in a saucepan over low heat, stirring frequently to prevent sticking or burning. Add a splash of water or broth if needed to achieve the desired consistency.

By following these tips, you can enjoy biscuits and gravy for lunch and dinner, and make the most of any leftovers with creative makeovers. Plus, you'll be able to freeze and reheat these dishes for quick and convenient meals throughout the week.

In this chapter, we've explored creative ways to enjoy biscuits and gravy beyond breakfast, including lunch and dinner ideas, leftover makeovers, and freezing and reheating tips. With these ideas, you can savor the comfort of biscuits and gravy throughout the day and week in the "Biscuits and Gravy Cookbook."

Thank You